The Laughing Trout

by

JIM URE

Copyright by 2012 by James W. Ure
All rights reserved.

Published by

Gardner & Grace Publishers

702 11th Avenue, Salt Lake City, UT 84103

www.jimurebooks.com

ISBN-10: 1481005324

EAN-13: 9781481005326

Library of Congress Control Number: 2012914597
CreateSpace Independent Publishing Platform
North Charleston, South Carolina

No part of this book may be reproduced in any form or by any means, graphic, electronic or mechanical, including photocopying, recording or by any storage retrieval system, without written permission of the author

This book is a work of fiction. Names, characters, places and incidents are either the product of the author's imagination or are used fictitiously, and any resemblance to actual persons, living or dead, business establishments and events and locales is entirely coincidental.

PRAISE (SOME OF IT FAINT) FOR *THE LAUGHING TROUT*

"A good fish story is in the telling ... and the humor. James Ure may turn out to be the best story teller of the decade."
~ Carolyn Howard-Johnson, multi award-winning novelist and poet

"As we all know, all trout fishing books are *fiction*. This one by Ure is just honest about it! This is a book every fly fisherman, needs to have handy. It's a book you'll return to whenever you start to take yourself too seriously–whenever you need a good laugh."
~ Bob Springmeyer
President, Bonneville Research
Editor, North Country Fishing Report 2008

"*The Laughing Trout* is well-written lunacy, something between Hunter Thompson and Tom Robbins."
~Dave Hall, artist

"My friend, the author, paints both beautiful and comic images alike with great style and panache. He describes one of my favourite places on the planet, the Henry's Fork of the Snake river at Last Chance Idaho, with mouth-watering and wrist-twitching accuracy ... .and when you read of the log fire ' ... sending sparklets into the Pleiades' you just know you're in for a visual treat."
~Franz Grimley Scottish river guide par excellence, Scottish River National Fly Fishing champion and Scottish

International and World championship team member and former team manager.

    www.Scottishfishingguides.co.uk

"This book has some profanity and some sex stuff in it that I don't like one bit."

~Helen B. Ure, author's mother.

Drawing by the late Sheridan M. Anderson, Courtesy Yvon Chouinard. Drawing is the result of a fishing contest between them and lost by Sheridan.

Cover art by Jim Hayes Jim@ha-yes.com
www.ha-yesdesign.com

Many Thanks

...to my father who had me dancing with eagerness to the tune of his Yellowstone fishing stories. And my mother, God bless her, who patiently delivered my to the fishing holes of my youth. So did Mr. Arbuckle, who recognized a fellow fishing devotee and hauled me to Deer Creek on many a Saturday.

Thanks to the men and women I have fished with and loved, especially my brother Joe and my son Cory.

My fly fishing tutelage began under Sheridan Anderson and was improved and enhanced by Raymond Leonhardt, Bob Springmeyer, Dave Hall, Peter Coombs, Pete and Rachel Taylor, Judy Martin, Steve Schmidt, Bob Tusken, Mike Lawson, Tom Grimes and Franz Grimley. Best of all were the friendships that came out of those lovely days on the river.

My thanks to Lavina Fielding Anderson for her editing, although my preefrooder, Roy Hobbs, may have made some errors while editing her revisions. They are his mistakes, not hers, and certainly not those of the author.

I also want to express deepest affection for the Provo, Millcreek, the Snake (both the Henry's Fork and the South Fork), the Tweed, the River Ure in Yorkshire, Big Cottonwood Creek, Rio Manso, Rio Limay, the Yellowstone, Gallatin, Rock Creek, Clark Fork and the Missouri, nameless lakes in the high Uintah Mountains, and of course, Curtis Creek. They taught me how to fish.

To the town of Rexburg, especially its high school band, I offer apologies for abusing the good nature of this fine community.

I thank Jim Hayes for the thoughtful work he put into the cover design.

*To the memory of Sheridan A. M. Anderson,
who drowned in dreams of Curtis Creek.*

Day One
Island Park, Idaho

CHAPTER ONE

Jud Buckalew

Jud Buckalew moved cautiously and slowly across the Snake River, allowing only his head to show above the riffles. The evening sun threw long shadows across the moving water. Beneath the blue-green flow, his naked body shone milk white.

Jud crouched low, pushing himself against the current with the tips of his toes. With his right hand, he reached down and felt the stringers of moss and the pebbles of the river bottom. In his left, he held a six-weight fly rod, letting it trail in the water behind him.

The run was less than four feet deep here at Last Chance. The pool for which Jud aimed lay in a slight calm at the head of a riffle, still nearly fifty yards away. He moved so slowly that it would be fifteen minutes before he would be in position to make a single cast to The Pig. He would get just one cast, for the huge rainbow had developed river-wisdom born of being sought by a thousand fishermen. Jud Buckalew had

The Laughing Trout

seen the swirls in the pool from his cabin window as he talked on the phone. He had quickly hung up, grabbed his rod, and headed for the river.

Three times Jud had hooked this fish. Each time she was surface feeding, which occurred infrequently at best.

Now The Pig was slurping pale morning duns off the surface with the relish of a Roman emperor sucking grapes at an orgy.

Jud had tried fishing down to the pool. He had tried from the sides. Only an approach from below—made difficult by the swift water—had produced results. And with the morning shadows low and long, he had to immerse himself almost entirely to keep from spooking her. The water swirled over Jud's chin and mouth and into his nose. He inched forward. Jud thought he heard someone calling, but the rush of water past his ears nullified the sound.

It came louder. His name. Jud took his eyes from the distant pool and looked toward the bank.

Hallooing at him, hands around her mouth, was his mother, Melba Willey Buckalew. She had come to the wilds of Henry's Fork wearing high heels, with a lilac dress and a matching hat perched atop her blue-white hair, reminding him of the nineteenth-century Englishwomen who carried parasols on partridge drives. A familiar uneasiness crept into Jud Buckalew's stomach. The old lady always did that.

He rose from his crawl, moss streaming from his legs and chest, water cascading from his body to reveal his nakedness. He saw his mother clap her hand to her mouth as he lost his balance and splashed back into the sturdy pull of the river, bouncing downstream several yards.

"That does it," he muttered, looking back at the pool as he struggled toward shore. The slurping fish no longer slurped.

Jud Buckalew

"Well, Ma. How are you? What brings you here?" he said levelly as he swept the water from his lean frame with the palm of his calloused hand.

Bob, a huge, tailless Manx cat, was curled up on the pile of his clothes. Jud pulled on his jeans and reached for his shirt. The cat tried to remain on the warm bundle, much as tableware tries to remain when the tablecloth is whisked away. Then Bob disdainfully moved into the grass and stretched his raven-black pelage before setting to a serious licking of his privates.

"Are you decent now?" she asked, turning around.

"Yeah, Ma. I'm decent." He pulled the yellow turtleneck over his head. Jud leaned over to let the water drain from each ear as his mother began.

"The Coyles are taking me to their cabin at Hebgen for the weekend. Mr. Coyle had some real estate business with someone up by Mack's Inn so I told him to drop me at your cabin. He's going to pick me up in a little while. I just wanted to say hello." She paused. He didn't answer.

"Humph," she sniffed. "You still have that cat. You're skinny. Don't you eat well?" The flowers on her lilac hat bounced as she machine-gunned him with words. Time and gravity had created jiggling jowls and massive breasts. Her face was petulant, unsmiling.

"I eat real well, Ma," said Jud patiently. It's just that working the river every day keeps me slendered-out." Was there ever a time she could say anything positive, he wondered? After thirty-nine years of criticism, maybe someday…

His thought was interrupted. "How's your business?" she asked.

"So-so. I've got a pretty good schedule this month but July and August aren't even a quarter filled. Some September regulars, though. What's new in Paris, Ma?"

The Laughing Trout

"Oh, it's been kind of exciting. Cattle prices have been good, and the spring raspberries came on real good. Your uncle has done quite well again, I must say."

Jud sniffed. His uncle, Bernard Bosham, would always do well. He was not only the largest landholder in Paris, Idaho, but had sold the world's smallest pony at least a dozen times. He bred small ponies on his Paris farms, under the brand name Tiny Trotters. He also bought and sold livestock, produce, hay, and grain.

She continued: "The town's started a tourist program. For all the visitors that come to Bear Lake, most of them go to Fish Haven. So we are putting up a sign over Main Street. It's going to say either '700 Parisians Can't Be Wrong' or 'Stay and Play an Extra Day.'"

"What are they gonna do for a day? You only got one cafe and a drugstore?" Jud pulled on his boots.

"You grew up in Paris; you know there's lots to do, Judson. They can boat on Bear Lake or visit the bird refuge, or of course there's fishing and hunting. Lots of people buying second homes along the west shore. It's downright crowded now," she said.

"Every place is crowded now, Ma," Jud observed, looking toward the Tetons where the sun was burnishing the range the color of trout flesh, trout flesh he would not see this night.

"There's some other news." Mrs. Buckalew began cautiously. Her tone snapped Jud out of his Teton reverie. He looked at her. It was a kind of warning note, an overture to sensitive matters about to be discussed.

"Your cousin Mark has been assigned by Idaho Game and Fish to work up here, in Island Park," she said quietly, looking down at the bank grass.

"Shit!" Jud hissed.

"Judson!" snapped his mother, looking up with fire in her eyes. She reminded him of an operatic Teuton hurling lightning bolts. "You WILL NOT use that language!"

"Oh, Ma. You know how I feel about Mark." Jud felt the anger in his cheeks.

"Stop that. He's my sister's son, your own flesh and blood. You be nice to him. Promise?" she said, putting liver-spotted hands on his damp shoulders.

His cousin was a bigger ass than his uncle.

Uncle Bernard played the dumb farmer and had slyly become the richest man in Paris. His son, Mark, had added obsequiousness to slyness, moving slowly, purposefully, with a stiletto smile fixed on his lips. But Jud's passionate dislike for Mark Bosham went even deeper, back to a time Jud didn't like to remember.

Jud dropped his battered Stetson on his head. Like a trained animal, the Stetson settled to the tan line just above his brows.

Led by the twenty-pound cat, the lady in lilac leaned on the tall fisherman as they walked slowly up the trail to the cabin in the pines.

"I brought you a lemon pie. Oh, yes. I found the ribbons from that dance contest in a shoebox in my closet. Do you remember that?" she said, laughing.

Jud smiled. Sometimes he forgot his mother's soft, more vulnerable qualities.

A bull moose fed in the lily pads of an old oxbow, his winter coat still clinging raggedly to his flanks.

Pushing above the pine-pointed skyline was a new moon.

The Pig rose silently. There was the underwater mirror-flash. The sail of a huge dorsal was exposed for an instant. A swirl. A large moth poured down the gullet of the big

The Laughing Trout

rainbow. Sinking to the bottom of the pool, the powerful trout moved to her customary resting place beneath a ledge of rock. She hugged it so tightly that her right pectoral fin was sandpapered to a ragged edge from constant fanning against the quartzite.

In this pool she had spent twenty summers. As pools go, it was deceptive. The rocks at its head formed nearly invisible water pillows, behind which the churning current had carved a narrow, deep run. Six feet deep in summer, the pool was flanked on either side by fifty yards of three-foot deep water. No breaking water marked her grotto. Occasionally a fishermen dropped into it unawares, only to rise flailing and sputtering amid flotsam from his vest, leaving a small flotilla bobbing away downstream—a hat and fly floatant, leader packets, plastic boxes of blue winged olives and Hemingway caddis.

As a fingerling the rainbow had found her way from her natal gravel and down a tiny tributary to Elk Creek and the Buffalo River. She had survived herons, snakes, and even the maw of her own father as she hovered in the shallows, always facing into the current, feeding on microorganisms.

At six inches and in her second year, she boldly moved into main current of the Buffalo, joining thousands of other small fish in an amorphous formation of trout in holding water. Now there were osprey and kingfishers to fear. It was here the female developed some life-long aversions. The Buffalo, being a good river for young human fishers, taught her about badly-presented streamers, worms, and dry flies of every pattern. She once was hooked on a tiny Mepps spinner, breaking free just as a kid was about to flop her onto the shore.

Her schoolroom training complete and her size now greater than the Buffalo could comfortably accommodate in its slow, shallow pools, she worked downstream and into the fast, deep water of Henry's Fork—also called the North Fork—of the Snake River. On a brittle-cold December day she drifted into the pool at Last Chance.

As she grew, she fed more and more on small trout and whitefish. She reserved one quirk, even after these many years: a penchant for occasional surface feeding.

This partiality might have killed her early on, for fly fishermen regularly plied the waters at Last Chance. But her predilection was based on a phenomenon of sorts. Just above her pool, a large boulder of pink quartzite thrust from the water, its angle such that it collected against its upstream surface the floating corpses of dead mayflies, beetles, flying ants, spinners and caddies. Frequently this collection of insect flotsam would be splashed loose by a particularly strong surge of river current, sending a small raft of insects directly into the feeding lane of the female. She learned to rise and gulp down this chitinous stew in two or three gentle slurps. Her palate thus whetted, she would feed for a few minutes on passing surface creatures. Then she would sink beneath her ledge to waylay small fish. She might not rise again for days.

She had a pearl eye as large as a quarter. Even in the deep, dark bottom of the hole, it was luminous and wise.

CHAPTER TWO

Mark Pays a Visit

His mother's last words that evening were, "Pray for Mark."

"I'll pray for Mark," said Jud Buckalew aloud to Bob. The cat tried to curl around his ankles as he scored the fat on a T-bone steak.

"I'll pray he falls into a stump shredder."

Jud irritably plunged garlic slivers into the maroon slab of meat. Mark Harvey Bosham was coming here.

He should have told his mother what was *really* on his mind, and he was vexed with himself for not speaking out. It always happened this way, his mother bullying him to carry out her wishes. Ever since childhood, he had gone to exasperating lengths to please her. She had been most pleased when he accomplished "things"—things like being the valedictorian of the Montpelier High School's graduating class and finishing his college degree. Everybody said Jud was smart and was going places. Good lookin', too, they said. But her acknowledgement of his accomplishments dissipated

The Laughing Trout

completely after what the town called "Jud's incident." Now she treated him like a child, and nothing he could say or do could compensate. She visited him dutifully but made it clear that he was still the subject of wagging tongues back in Paris.

Melba Buckalew held Mark Bosham up to Jud as an inspiration, in spite of the fact that she had a pretty clear idea why Jud had come to despise Mark. Mark had, after all, a master's degree, and was a successful wildlife manager for the state. When asked, she said her son was "Just a fishing guide." Jud flopped the steak onto the charcoal grill. Adjusting the grill until the timbre of the sizzle was just right, he settled into the porch chair. Bob jumped on the rail and rested, eyes half shut, on his belly.

Jud sipped coffee and looked down at the Snake River's black water, spangled here and there by silver-flecked riffles. The steady flow of the river hissed in his ears.

Might be two or three more days before the salmon fly hatch worked its way up to this part of the river. He had tied plenty of salmon flies. Jud turned the steak and watched it sizzle against the cherry-orange coals. He should start tying caddis on number eighteen and twenty hooks tonight. Maybe some hare's ears nymphs. When the salmon flies dropped off, the fishermen he guided would be looking for other patterns. He knew the rainbows of the Snake would begin hitting big goldens, caddis, and drakes just four or five days after the salmon fly hatch ended. And he sold those flies to his parties on the river. Everyone he guided paid for a dozen flies, whether he used them or not.

Buckalew forked the grid-marked steak onto his plate.

The mosquitoes were active now, so he went inside. He set the plate on the gingham patterned oilcloth of his table, turned off the overhead light, and lit a candle. The polished pine walls glowed like warm brass in the candlelight. Jud was

Mark Pays a Visit

proud of his little cabin. He'd acquired it almost by chance after fleeing to Island Park from the nightmare in Paris. It had been the hardest time of his life. No money. No wife. Not a friend in the world. And a lot of pain.

When he arrived at Island Park, Jud at first camped at a little spring on Stamp Meadow Road. He flagellated himself with his past sins for two weeks, staying dry through sheer will power and feeling as ragged and mean as a rusty power saw. Then he found those Saturday night A.A. meetings at the Chapel of the Pines at Mack's Inn.

It was hard, at first, admitting he had a problem. But he felt better after he talked at the meetings. One night, a man named Oswald King came to him after a meeting "I hear you might need a place to live," said King. "I've got a framed-in cabin that needs some finish work. If you'll do the work, you can live there until you get on your feet."

A minor miracle, thought Jud at the time. He snapped at the chance and soon was plumbing, paneling, and painting. Meanwhile, he signed on as a guide with Yellowstone Country Anglers and a few dollars began trickling in.

A year later Jud took the plunge, bought a drift boat, and hung up his own guide's shingle, sometimes hiring out to other outfitters, including his old one. Winters he spent doing remodeling work for the cabin owners whose places dotted Highway 20 from Ashton, Idaho, to West Yellowstone, Montana. Sometimes during winter, he'd take a break and, breasting the icy waters of the Madison or the Snake, he'd catch whitefish on tiny flies. He then smoked them and frequently ate smoked white fish for breakfast, as one might eat kippers in England.

His life slowly, steadily got better. One night after the A.A. meeting King offered to sell Jud the cabin. The payments were low at first, to be increased as Jud's business

The Laughing Trout

grew. The cabin had a large kitchen-living area on the main floor, two bedrooms up, and a loft to store his junk in. Jud grabbed at it. He sliced a chunk of steak for Bob and put it on a plate on the table. The cat jumped up and began purr-growling like an outboard motor as his big fangs worried the beef. Quietly munching, Jud listened to the Snake River in the darkness.

His thoughts went back to his mother's visit. For a family to stick together was the most important thing for Melba Buckalew.

"You never know when you will need family," she always warned. When his father died, Uncle Bernard Bosham had magnanimously offered Melba a job keeping his books at minimum wage, and Melba to this day believed the man a saint. His cousin, Mark Harvey Bosham, was cut from the same cloth as his old man: he was a taker. And a prick, Jud added with satisfaction as he washed the dinner plates. He settled into the big, wooden rocking chair by the picture window. He felt soothed and satisfied with the cat and the light of the candle. He gently stroked Bob. It was quiet except for the sibilance of the river below. The night was still. He heard the fluting of a distant sandhill crane. The cat was the first to notice the aroma. Bob, curled in Jud's lap, lifted his head and sniffed. His yellow eyes narrowed. Jud smelled it. Sweet, familiar, yet repugnant. He heard footfalls in the duff of the trail. Thumps on the cabin porch.

"Hello, anybody home?" came a familiar, high-pitched nasal voice. Looking through the screen from behind a very large, very ornate Meerschaum pipe, was a cunningly cherubic face with rosy round cheeks and bushy black beard. Fixed in place was a steely smile, looking like the grille of a pickup truck. The eyes were empty and eerie, like a house with a power outage. This was Mark Harvey Bosham. The

Mark Pays a Visit

cat growled a fate motif. Jud blinked his eyes in disbelief. Bosham walked into the cabin without invitation, leading with the pipe, which drooled the smoky fragrance they had smelled.

Jud Buckalew did not rise from the rocker.

"Hello, hello, Cousin Juddy," said Mark, smiling that fixed smile, shaking a brown bottle. He saw the cat.

"You? With a cat? I don't believe it."

"Yup," said Jud.

"I brought Scotch whiskey. I thought we could have a little drink and have a little talk," said Mark, his face smiling yet expressionless.

"I won't drink with you, Mark." Jud knew his cousin would be undaunted.

"Well, then, let's have a friendly talk. Like the old days."

"Those days are past, Mark. I got nothin' to say to you."

"Are you still sore? C'mon now, Juddy. It's me, Mark, your cousin." Mark sat astride a kitchen chair.

In the candlelight Jud saw he was in his usual Western-cut shirt and corduroys. Jud sat back in the chair and waited for a moment before speaking: "I can barely be civil to you and only because I promised Melba I would be."

"Those are bygone days, Juddy. I won. It's simple," said Mark.

"That's an ugly goddamn way you view life," Jud spat, leaning forward in the rocker. "We were doing something we could both win at."

"You're jealous because I was the one that actually did *something*," said Mark, smiling innocently. "That's survival of the fittest, Juddy boy." He puffed on his pipe. The cat sneezed.

Mark continued: "You couldn't have done a damn thing anyway. Have you forgotten your little incident? Paris has not forgotten, I assure you. Then you disappeared."

Jud snorted derisively to hide his discomfort. It felt as if Mark was gripping his neck, making him peer into an outhouse hole at the sewage of his past. Jud reeled with the pain. It put a nail in his desire to argue.

"Jud," hissed Mark through his smile, "you're a drunk. That's why you never got anywhere."

Jud's eyes narrowed. He spoke slowly: "And that's why you brought a bottle? Just like always. Get Jud drunk and he'll give you anything he's got, including his soul?" His voice dropped to a lower register. Get out of here, Mark."

"We can't avoid each other," said smiling Mark Bosham, standing. "I just wanted to be friendly."

"Friendly, my ass. That's over," said Jud, rising from his chair. "I can never trust you. I should have stopped trusting you when you killed The Battleship. You manipulate and lie and cheat. We may be blood relatives but we are not friends."

The smile fell abruptly from Mark's face as he tugged at his beard and looked sharply at Jud.

"I got some *authority* in Island Park now and you just happen to need a license from me in order to work. Don't try to make any trouble," he said, the truck grille smile returning.

"Ah. Blackmail. Now that's more like the old Mark I remember," Jud said. "There's the door."

Mark smiled at him levelly, trying to think of something more to say. He nodded, turned, slammed the screen door behind him, and stomped off the porch.

Jud sat in the darkness. Bob climbed back into his lap. He stroked the cat and sorted his feelings. He had angered his cousin. That worried him at first. He had been brought up to be a pleaser.

"I think I did the right thing, Bob," he said. He could see sparks as he stroked the thick, black fur. He thought: Oh, hell, I'm letting this resentment eat at me. It doesn't do any

Mark Pays a Visit

good to be angry any more. Yet Mark is such a prick. And now he's back in my life again. The rocker creaked like a new shoe. If only he could throw off these feelings and get on with life. His anger was as much for letting himself be used as it was at his cousin for using him.

"What I really need is a catharsis. I need to puke the past up and get on with today," he said to Bob as they climbed the stairs to the loft and the bed with its big down comforter. It would be cold before dawn.

Jud lay awake for a long time.

CHAPTER THREE

The Lago Poopo Trout

The first rays of sunlight speared through the pines as Jud Buckalew wiped a dab of shaving cream from the cleft in his chin and rinsed his angular face in the basin. He growled at the crow's feet in the corners of the river-blue eyes. The white of his forehead was a beacon in contrast to the weather-beaten tan of his capable face. He combed his shower-damp hair back over his ears and looked once again at the gray at his temples. He did not like getting old, but some things about him were holding up well, he noted, sucking through his perfect teeth. They were refrigerator-white. And his body was still hard and lean from days behind the oars.

The telephone rang. He jumped down the stairs from the bathroom loft in three leaps, sliding along the handrails in a controlled fall. Still a kid at heart, he thought, picking up the phone from its wall mount over the kitchen table.

"Jud Buckalew Guide Service."

The Laughing Trout

"Mr. Buckalew," said a not-quite-familiar voice. "I saw your classified ad in "Trout and Fly Fishing" and I want to hire your services so I can lay in a year's supply of rainbow trouts for my freezer."

"If you want *fish*, not *fishing*, I can recommend someplace else, like your local market. It's a damn sight cheaper," snapped Jud.

"Relax, hardass. It's me. Pasko."

"Rollo Pasko! Man, it's good to hear your voice. Are you still in Stanley? "said Buckalew.

"Ooooooh, noooooo. Seems I pissed in the soup in Idaho. I am proud to say that I am in Maryland building fish for the U.S. Government. Patuxent, Maryland. I am calling you compliments of your tax money on a government line. Just kicking back with a cup of U.S. government coffee. Thought I'd get caught up on my old friend after I saw your ad."

"Wait a minute," interrupted Jud. "Fill me in. It's been seven years since I saw you. We were very drunk at the Sawtooth Chapter Fisheries Convention in Boise. Didn't you have a fish farm at Hell Roaring Lake working under an agreement with Idaho F and G on some kind of commercial aquaculture venture?"

"Yeah. Hell of a deal. We were releasing fish like crazy into the lake as fingerlings. We were harvesting a nice batch when they returned to spawn in the hatchery traps in the spring," said Rollo Pasko laconically.

"Sounds perfect."

"It was a good deal till I fell in love with the commercial side of the business. The money. See, I'd release the trout and let them feed until they reached some size in the lake. Saved the cost of farm-feeding trout. Then they'd come back to the farm to spawn in the spring. I hired a dozen locals and we'd harvest, clean and quick-freeze them. We were getting a dollar a pound, and the first year I made an indecent amount of money," said Rollo Pasko.

"My agreement was to allow all the sport fishermen who fished in Hell Roaring Lake to keep the legal limit of all the trout they caught. Those guys were allowed to keep anything they could catch. See, the idea was that it would be good for me as a commercial operator to have the state's lake provide fish food. Sort of like grazing cattle on public land? And then the license-holding sportsmen could harvest some of the fish I planted," said Pasko.

"Clever," said Jud, shifting the phone as he sat down.

"The sportsmen didn't think so. Seems their fishing got worse. A lot worse. My harvests got better. Sportsmen investigated. I lost my contract."

"Okay, Rollo. Why did you lose the contract?" coaxed Jud.

"They had spies. They saw me shocking my fingerlings," said Rollo.

"Shocking your fingerlings?"

"Yeah. Before I'd release 'em, I'd throw worms and lures into the growing pens and when the fingerlings would go for 'em, I'd give the little bastards an electric shock. You only have to do that once or twice, and they'll never again go for worms or lures. That way I got to harvest more," said Rollo. "The worm and lure guys just weren't catching any fish."

Jud had a picture of Rollo Pasko throwing electrical switches and cackling like the mad scientist he was trained to be. He could see his red hair and freckled face as clearly as the day they met at Utah State University.

"Say," said Rollo. "I hear you cleaned up your act. You happy?"

"I did. And yeah, things are pretty good for me now. I've got a simple life and no money. Nice little three-room cabin,

The Laughing Trout

a drift boat, a pickup and a Manx cat," said Jud, his mind wandering back to the mirror image of crow's feet in the corner of his eyes.

"No woman? What happened to the gorgeous redhead you married."

"Beth? She's living somewhere in Oregon, I hear," said Jud.

"Hell, she was a terrific woman. I thought you and she were forever."

"Too much booze and then there was this...situation. The marriage couldn't stand it," said Jud slowly.

"What kind of situation?" said Rollo.

"That's something I don't feel like talking about. How's Ellie?"

Rollo paused for a moment. "She's living in San Diego with Sam and Christy. I talk to them all the time. She went south when all my fish earnings dropped precipitously. She wanted money. We do desperate things in the pursuit of sex," sighed Pasko.

"Everything does, Rollo. Robins break their necks flying into windows chasing sex. Male spiders get eaten after screwing. Now what's this fish-building business?" said Jud idly.

"Oh, yeah. Well, I saw a federal government opening for a fisheries biologist with experience in aquaculture and mitochondrial DNA work. Right up my alley. I says to myself: Self, this is for you. I answered the ad and here I am."

"What exactly are you doing, Rollo?" asked Jud. Holding the phone, he filled a cup with coffee from the enamel pot steaming on the stove.

"Actually, I am attached to the State Department—"

"The State Department," laughed Jud. "You, in a pinstripe suit?"

"American fish deserve the best. You want me to look good for them don't you? As I was saying, my work is in

The Lago Poopo Trout

creating species of fish that America can give to underdeveloped countries to help them create an aquaculture system to boost their economy. We figure out what kind of fish will grow best in a given lake in Uganda or Ceylon and then we can provide a strain of fish with the genetics built into it to survive and thrive.

"They harvest them, their economy improves. Foreign country is America's friend forever," said Rollo.

"Hey. I like it. So you can create a super-perch or a cross between a tilapia and a carp," said Jud. "Sounds kind of nifty."

"Most of the time, it is. Sometimes we get our genes spliced wrong and wind up with Lago Poopo trout," said Rollo, laughing.

Jud couldn't help laughing with him, even as he asked, "What the hell is a Lago Poopo trout?"

"There's this lake in Bolivia called Lago Poopo, and they wanted a specialized trout that would live in its high-altitude waters that had a certain chemical, mineral, and biomass soup. Okay, I says, taking out my test tubes," said Pasko.

"But I spliced the wrong genes and got a batch of very weird trout out of the eggs. It was a real fuck-up, I must say. My boss threatened to stuff one and hang it on the wall as a reminder," added Rollo Pasko.

"What was it like?" said Jud curiously.

"Now, get this: Absolutely toothless lower jaw. Two very large fangs on the upper jaw. The only teeth the fish had. It had spiny pectoral fins that were almost as strong as those of a catfish. I mean, really evil-looking devils. It had a very small eye and large nostrils. The tail was as square as a rainbow's except for a tiny upper spine. You know, like you see on swordtails? And then it had an internal diaphragm structure that reminded me very much of some of the reef

The Laughing Trout

fish that can use a diaphragm to boom out ultra-low frequency sound to stun their prey. Had an absolutely perfect, trout-like adipose fin. Lovely color, just like a Bonneville cutthroat. I even grew half a dozen up to two pounds in size to see what their behavior would be. Named them Lethargy, Ennui, Apathy, Sloth, Slug, and Dolt. Tell you something about their behavior?" queried Rollo.

"I guess they wouldn't take dry flies?" said Jud.

"They were most partial to Cheez Whiz. Say, how's your asshole cousin? I haven't seen his self-promoting press releases in the Fisheries Bulletins lately," said Rollo.

"Same sweet Mark. Unfortunately he has just been assigned to Island Park. Between him and my fear that I will never be immortal, I've had a couple of bad days," said Jud.

"You ain't forty yet?"

"In August. Yet I'm better at everything now than I was at twenty. It's just that I'm starting all over. No legacy and all that bullshit. You know. Hell, maybe you *don't* know," Jud added.

"I kind of know. But I've got two kids. You sound like you're wallowing in self-pity," said Rollo with the ruthlessness that comes only with being an old friend.

"It's just that Mark's arrival here brought back some old memories I want to forget," said Jud, drifting into thought.

Rollo continued chattering.

The conversation had given Jud an idea. He did not want to think that what he was feeling was revenge, exactly.

But he knew he could enjoy watching Mark make a fool of himself.

He interrupted his friend.

"Hey, Rollo. You keep any of those Lago Poopo trout? said Jud.

"Only a few in stiff repose in the deep freeze," answered Rollo.

"What are you going to do with them?"

"Throw 'em out. Freezer's full of other more important samples."

"How about sending them to me? I know someone who could use a jolt of Dolt," said Jud.

"Jud, I dunno. These are laboratory experiments. If my department ever found they'd been let out of this restricted lab, I'd be in deep feces," said Rollo.

"No one will ever know. I want 'em as a joke. Just send me three of them," said Jud. "Pack 'em in dry ice and ship 'em air freight. Great way to clean the freezer," Jud said.

"For you, Jud? Okay. But nobody can know where they came from. And you'll be sure to give them a proper burial? I grew kind of fond of them," said Rollo. "Hell, it's nine o'clock here. I better get back to work. Sure good talking to you Jud. Glad you're healthy and reasonably happy. I'll get back out to see you next year maybe."

"Good to hear from you, Rollo. Send the fish to me care of The Laughing Trout Bar and Grill.

CHAPTER FOUR

Vera

Jud pulled into the parking lot at Vera's Laughing Trout Bar and Grill. He sniffed pine smoke in the cool morning air. Before him stood a low, log lodge with a shake roof, its bay window hung with six unlighted neon beer signs. A bar is a lonely-looking place in the morning sun, he thought. His heels crunched through the gravel of the parking area as he walked past Vera Segura's big Chevy van. Jud smiled as he noted the clear plastic bug screen running the width of the grill, with its words YENROH ER'UOY FI KNOH. Beal Finnegan had put it on backward at his service station and Vera took such perverse pleasure in reminding him of the error that she had not yet let him reinstall it properly.

Behind the building, toward the Snake River, stood eight one-room log guest cabins. An oval wood sign hung from mounts under the porch of the lodge:

Laughing Trout Steaks Spirits Cabins

The Laughing Trout

"Mornin', Vera," said Jud as he strode through the door and up to the bar.

"Mornin', Jud," said Vera Segura, flashing her broad smile.

"Love your hair gizmos," said Jud, nodding toward the enamel chopsticks she was wearing to keep her thick black hair in its loose bun on the back of her head. Her flashing, combative brown eyes gave no hint of age; what Vera lacked in leg, she more than made up in bust. She was dressed in jeans and a pink V-neck sweater. A cross dangled at her throat. Her lipstick was coral pink, standing out starkly against her deep tan face.

Jud slid onto a stool and looked around the restaurant and bar. It was typical of a Western roadhouse.

Some booths, tables, and chairs, all chrome and leatherette with a tatterdemalion past. A wall of quick-food grocery snacks, stocked once each spring, already down to a single pack of Oreos but abundant with canned pineapple and Campbell's Vegetable Soup. A cooler of beer and wine. Shelves of whiskey behind a bar. A tack board flagged with scraps of paper, notes and signs, snapshots and cards.

Through an opening was the kitchen behind the bar.

Over the bar was a sign: WELCOME TO IDAHO, WHERE MEN ARE MEN AND SHEEP ARE NERVOUS.

The booths in the neonless morning gloom were empty. The remains of fire from last night smoked lazily in the big rock fireplace. Out the back window, Jud could see the river rolling by. He pulled a copy of the Idaho Falls *Post Register* toward him and began to read.

"Tell me it ain't so, Juddy," said Vera as she poured his coffee, her brown eyes mischievously glancing up.

"What ain't so?" Jud peered over the top of the paper.

"That you ain't got a cousin named Mark who is now the official fish cop for Island Park," said Vera.

Jud sipped the hot coffee. "Guilty. But not responsible. What'd he do?"

"Came in last night. There were a couple of schoolteachers from Salt Lake having dinner. He started to hit on 'em. I've never heard such bullshit," said Vera. "You want breakfast?"

"Yeah. Huevos," Jud said, putting the paper aside.

"Mark must have come over here after he found I was lousy company."

"Torts or toast."

"Torts."

"He had this big, phony pipe. He'd take a puff and then strike a pose and quote famous poets so loud the whole bar could hear," said Vera as she scraped the griddle. "He couldn't seem to shut up."

"Did he say 'I know only what is moral is what you feel good after and what is immoral is what you feel bad after'?" asked Buckalew.

"Something like that. Several times. Told them he was born and raised in Paris and didn't come to the States till he was twelve," she scoffed, breaking the eggs. She slapped a flat of hash browns on the griddle.

"That's my cousin. Sometimes he finds someone who speaks French and then he's in trouble," Jud added. "What did the women do?"

"One may have been impressed right out of her panties. They left together. The other made a face and stayed to talk with me and Mort. She told us your cousin was just another horny con artist," Vera added. Laramie Mort was Vera's night bartender.

"Gotta watch out for Mark. He'll use that line about 'feeling the earth move out and away from under you' and you'll be mighty impressed," chuckled Jud, resuming his newspaper.

"Hey! I nearly forgot," said Vera brightly.

The Laughing Trout

There's a package for you. It came yesterday. You were on the river so the express truck driver left it here." Vera plunged out of sight in the back room. Jud heard the freezer door clank shut. Vera, curious, gossipy, might want to know what the package contained.

"There," said Vera, placing the box on the floor at the end of the counter. "Oh, hey. Your eggs."

The box was from Rollo Pasko. Jud smiled, thinking to tell the distracted Vera of his scheme, but then thought better of it. He had promised Rollo.

"What's in it?" she asked.

"Blue crabs from a friend in Maryland."

CHAPTER FIVE

The Old Switcheroo

Jud let the high-ended Mackenzie boat drift on the dark green slick as the current pushed them toward the north bank. He pulled on the left oar to correct course and give his angler a better position from which to cast at a run below a large rock.

"Below the rock, right next to the grassy overhang of the bank, Gary," Jud instructed. He was guiding a single fisherman, Gary Pollock, an easy-going, self-deprecating jewelry store owner from Encino, California. Gary cast well.

The salmon fly dropped where the little whitecaps met the curl of the blue-green eddy. CHOP. A swirl.

Gary's line snugged tight, his custom-made rod arced. A slab-sided rainbow tail-danced once, twice, thrice on the surface of the Henry's Fork, to the envy of any rodeo bronco.

"That's a nice fish," said Jud, backing water with the oars to let his fare have full play of the fish. Jud looked downstream a few hundred yards. He noted that next they would come to the Pig's Pool. Beyond that, he thought he could see Mark Bosham at the take-out, clipboard in hand, checking licenses and catches.

The afternoon sun blinked out intermittently as towering cumuli sailed over Island Park. The clouds would bring rain any time now.

"Keep your tip up," Jud suggested. Gary was pulling in line a few inches at a time. Jud grounded the boat in the shallows near the bank. The fish was tired, tailing in the water; one short dash was left in him. He made a twenty-five-foot run. Gary slowly turned him.

Jud unfurled the net. The fish was about two pounds. He scooped up the rainbow, holding it briefly as he removed the salmon fly from its lip.

"There's another rise," he said, pointing. "See that calm near the pink rock? Cast to that," he said.

As the fisherman false-cast, looking intently at the river, Jud allowed the rainbow to slide back into the current, where it quickly darted into the green darkness.

He quietly took an aluminum-foil package from the food cooler, opened its end, and allowed its contents to slide into the fish cooler. He looked up to see if he had been observed. Gary was casting intently. A chuckle rose in Jud's throat as he looked at the peculiar Lago Poopo trout stretched out in the cooler. He shut the lid and pulled on the oars once to straighten the boat.

They drifted toward the Pig's Hole slowly. Jud always had a difficult decision to make as he neared the deep run. When his day's trip was a fisherman of little talent, technique, or wisdom, it was easy to let him flail away at the hole. When in the service of a fine fisherman, Jud became circumspect. If the Pig belonged to anyone, it was his. It was the toughest animal he'd ever challenged. But what if, just what if, another fisherman actually hooked The Pig? Jud knew he would be devastated. When he arrived five years before and the big fish had risen to his fly after days and weeks of attempts, Buckalew had focused on his efforts to catch it as a way of neutralizing the memory of the wreckage of his past. Each time he approached the Pig, it was different, challenging. The big rainbow became the gauge against which he measured his growth since he had become sober. It represented his new-found discipline and courage. It brought him new patience. His self-esteem was reborn as Jud's old can-do returned. The Pig had taught Jud something about accepting life on life's terms rather than on self-will and manipulation.

The boat slowly swung into position above the hole.

"There's a good size trout in that hole," said Jud, watching his fisherman's face. "Keep your fly toward this side and do your best to keep your leader tippet in the rougher water. Do you want to put on more leader?"

"Naw. I'll go with this," said Gary, shooting the line forward. Jud's disquiet over the Pig eased as he saw the line overshoot the pocket and plop noisily in the slick water, a curl of leader kinked a few inches above the fly. If The Pig had been feeding near the surface, the clatter of the presentation had sent her deep beneath the cut-away rock ledge. The man cast three more times.

On a third cast another two-pound rainbow sucked in the fly. Gary's face lit up with pleasure. Gary never knew,

Large, scattered drops of rain were falling when the boat scraped onto the gravel bar at Last Chance. Mark Bosham came toward them, clipboard in hand.

The Laughing Trout

"Hello, Jud," smiled Mark Bosham perfunctorily, warily. "May I see your fishing license, driver's license and any fish you may have kept, please."

Gary produced his licenses. Jud opened the fish cooler and shoved it toward Mark.

"Thank you," said Mark, handing Gary's wallet back to him.

Mark sorted through the three fish allowed under the current slotting allotment, noting on his clipboard the species and size.

Jud watched an osprey beating toward the north with a head-forward fish in its talons. His back was to Mark when he heard him say: "Holy shit. What is this!" There was a twisted, gargling sound in Mark's voice, as if he were swallowing a large ice cube. The truck grille smile was there, looking bizarre under the circumstances.

Jud turned and innocently said: "What is *what?*"

"Look at this, wouldya? What do you make of it?"

Mark held up a Lago Poopo trout.

"Sure has a small eye." Jud paused, turning the fish as he inspected it. "Look at the jaw," he said.

"Nice color. Adipose fin. Definitely a trout."

"Look at the tail," said Mark.

"Strange. Didn't notice it when we landed him. Must have been the one we caught at the end of the whitewater in Box Canyon. Did you notice it, Gary?"

"No," said the stunned angler, looking at his fish.

"It's, well, it's ... grotesque, isn't it?" He drew back from the fish.

"Just one of nature's freaks," said Jud.

"Probably," said Mark. "But I'm going to have to take the fish. For further study, you understand."

The Old Switcheroo

""I don't want it," said Gary, staring at the trout with wide eyes.

"Look at this," said Jud, fingering the pectoral fins. "Spiked and hard, like a catfish."

"Damn. What a weird fish," said Mark as he slid it into his cooler.

"No doubt a genetic accident," said Jud as he lifted gear from the boat.

"Yuk," said Gary. "I don't remember landing that."

CHAPTER SIX

The Second Lago Poopo Trout

Dear Mr. Fish Biologist: I was tole you wuod want to see this fish I cauwt below Coffee Pot rapid. Its a ugly fish.
   Yours Truly
   Peter Johnson

   Jud wrote the note in pencil with his left hand. Now the hand was cramped, being unused to writing.

   He took a second Lago Poopo trout and placed it in a plastic bag with ice. He taped the note over the bag and carefully bound the package with rubber bands. Jud slipped into the dusk.

   An hour later, he was back at his cabin. He lit a fire, fixed a cup of coffee, and read some Emerson with Bob curled in his lap. At 11:00 o'clock he stretched and decided to turn in.

The Laughing Trout

He had a trip in the morning and the guests wanted an early start. Jud had been asleep only a few minutes when a heavy thumping on his door awoke him and jarred Bob into a low, menacing growl.

"So soon?" Jud muttered to himself as he threw on his robe and ambled downstairs.

BAMBAMBAM.

"What is it, Mark?" he said, opening the inside door.

"It's important. You're the only person I can talk to about this," said Mark Bosham in harsh, low tones. He looked over his shoulders, as if there might be spies.

Jud was glad it was dark. In his sleepiness, he was having difficulty keeping a straight face. He wanted desperately to giggle.

"It can wait," said Jud.

"No. This is very, very big," whispered Mark. "Let me in."

Jud swung the door open. He turned on a light.

Mark immediately opened the package with the second Lago Poopo trout and laid it on Jud's table.

"This was left inside my screen door tonight when I was at dinner," said Mark, eyes wide.

"You mean this isn't the same one my party caught?" said Jud.

"No! A second one!" whispered Mark. "That could mean a strain, or race. A whole new species! Oncorhyncus mark bosham!"

"So the first was not just a single mutation," said Jud with solemnity. He stroked Bob.

"What do you make of this fish, Jud?" said Bosham.

This was the way Mark had always done it. He would ask for Jud's opinion, agree with it, then claim it as his.

"Well. It's got a tiny eye. Might mean it doesn't need an eye to feed. Or maybe it feeds only at night. It probably has a highly developed sensitivity to vibrations. So it doesn't need the eye. Who knows? Lots of research to do here, Mark," said Jud. "The other one sure hit my party's fly hard."

"Wow. An aggressive, blind trout!" said Mark. "What about the spiked pectorals," he asked slyly.

"That's easy. It uses them to hold itself to the bottom in these swift currents. Probably uses 'em like those walking catfish in Florida. They can pull themselves along with them. Might save metabolic expenditure," said Jud with gravity.

"That's it, all right," said Mark, smacking his fist into his open palm. "Now how do I find out where this thing originated? Genetically, I mean?"

"You could do some mitochondrial DNA research and learn something," said Jud.

"That's it. I'll send one of these off—" Mark began.

Jud interrupted. "It doesn't work that way. You must have living tissue," said Jud, yawning, not sure his cousin would accept this statement.

"Oh. I have to get a live one," said Bosham, nodding to himself. Mark was quiet for half a minute, looking off into the embers of the fireplace. Then he broke the silence.

"Jud. I've come up with something significant here. Do not tell a soul," said Mark, straightening in his chair, talking with a deep, important voice.

"I won't, Mark. I've got to hit the hay now." Jud walked to the door and held it open. Bob stretched.

Mark thumped across the porch and disappeared in the darkness.

Bob the cat was startled by the roar of laughter trailing after Jud as he climbed the stairs to bed.

CHAPTER SEVEN

Strike and Run

Jud trained the spotting scope on the Pig's Hole.

Mists were rising from the river in the still, dawn air.

"She rises, Bob." Jud took his rod from the wall hanger and quickly gulped the dregs of his first cup of coffee as he tied on a size sixteen olive caddis.

He was a quarter of a mile from the pool yet he softly shut the screen door of the cabin. Bob wove down the trail in front of him.

On the bank of the river, Jud shed his clothes and with a gasp climbed into the water. His scrotum instantly puckered, his testicles shrank to navy beans, and he was without breath for five seconds. Jud immersed himself to his neck and began making the slow crawl upriver to the feeding fish. He'd been right on the salmon flies. The hatch was over, and now perhaps the caddis would produce as it had done for his clients these last few days.

The Laughing Trout

He was carefully planning as he moved toward the dimples. Then he saw the wave of a great dorsal, and a swirl. She was feeding just below the surface. Had she been feeding on hatching larva, she'd have been deeper, Jud reasoned. No, he expected that last night's thunderstorm had loosened critters from their nocturnal perches and sent them spilling into the river. A hungry Pig was slurping up the protein flotsam as it drifted on or near the surface.

Ten minutes of slow crawling brought a numb Jud to within thirty feet of the feeding fish. He pushed ahead ever so slowly, moving each foot only a few inches, finding a hold, then slowly moving the other foot forward.

The fish still slurped. Jud rose above the water, silently stripping line from his reel, letting the caddis drift behind him as he gathered line in his left hand.

With a careful, single stroke, Jud shot the line forward, feeling the vibration as it cleared the rod-eyes and hissed toward the hole like a snake's tongue. The fly gently arced up and dropped on the water, the twelve-foot leader and line curving back into the chop of the current.

Jud fingered in slack with his hand, holding his breath. The undressed fly rode low on the water—three feet, four feet, five feet. Then it disappeared. Jud imagined it rolling just beneath the surface.

Jud saw a mirror flash in the blue-green water and struck before the line showed a hint of tug. He could feel the solid, shoulder-jarring lock of steel and bone.

Then he felt nothing. The line seemed to go slack. The big trout refused to believe itself hooked and had decided not to run. It sulked.

For a moment, Jud entertained the notion that the big trout might attack him. Naked, he felt utterly vulnerable."Now

Strike and Run

what?" he muttered. He pulled up slack until he had taken the belly out of the line. It felt like a snag—almost.

The Pig came directly at him in a rushing charge. The slack of the line gathered briefly at his side until the trout shot by, heading downstream at missile-speed. The reel shrieked as she picked up the slack and ripped of another dozen yards of line. In an instant she was into the backing and still charging downstream. The reel spool held a hundred yards of backing: Jud looked down to note that at least half the backing was gone and the fish showed no sign of slowing.

Rod tip high, he tried to break the run. For a second, the fish stopped, and Jud thought perhaps he had slowed her.

A great trout leaped downstream, thrashing the surface of the Snake with a shotgun-spray of droplets.

The last few feet of backing ripped from the reel. Jud felt the PUNG of tight line! Then it was slack. He reeled in the line slowly, his arms stiff, his fingers stinging. The end of the leader was snapped clean at the knot where it joined the hook. Jud was shaking. It wasn't from the cold.

CHAPTER EIGHT

In The News

"You okay?" said Vera, spinning a cup of coffee toward Jud as he settled uncertainly over a barstool.

"No. I am not. I hooked a big fish this morning and it left me shaken," Jud admitted as he reached for the morning paper.

"I heard there's a big one you're trying to catch. Somebody said you fish naked for it. Figure it'll go for the big worm? Or do you plan to screw it when you catch it?" Vera cackled as she poured hotcake batter on the griddle.

"It's my secret lure. Stop making fun of my venerable tool," said Jud.

"Oh, I could make some fun *with* your venerable tool," said Vera coquettishly. "Only the fish get to see it?"

"Someday, Vera, when you've prepared yourself physically and mentally, then I might unleash him," said Jud, snapping the newspaper flat. "Hello, what's this?" he asked before Vera could respond. On the front page was a photo of

Mark Harvey Bosham, pipe in mouth, an attempt at a scholarly look on his simpering face, displaying both of the Lago Poopo trout. Jud grinned as he read the story.

"Isn't that wonderful?" he said, turning the paper for Vera to read:

NEW TROUT IN SNAKE RIVER?

IDAHO FALLS, IDAHO (AP)—An unusual and possibly a new species of trout has been discovered in the Henry's Fork of the Snake River by an Idaho Fish and Game biologist.

The trout, which has small eyes, a large, undershot jaw, spiny pectoral fins, and fangs, was discovered near Last Chance in Island Park by Biologist Mark Harvey Bosham as he checked creels.

"This is a major find," announced Bosham after he called a press conference to unveil the fish. "Two of them have turned up in the past few days."

The "Bosham trout," as he calls it, may have some unusual behavioral characteristics.

"For instance, it may use its spines to anchor itself in the swift waters of the Snake," he said.

"We now need to find a live specimen of the Bosham trout in order to run the necessary tests to determine its origins and to see if it poses any hazard to populations of other trout species."

"This is the discovery of the century," says Bosham.

Jud finished the story.

"I'd say he's as full of shit as a baby bird," she muttered. "Oh, oh. Your hotcakes." She turned to the griddle.

CHAPTER NINE

Bob Helps

The dory drifted toward Last Chance. Jud's guest lost his grip on an eighteen-inch rainbow, and the fish was thrashing in the gear at their feet.

"Do you want to keep this one?" asked Jud.

"Yes, I do," said the fisherman, a plump gray-haired man from Seattle. He tried again to scoop up the fish from the deck. It flopped away.

On this afternoon, Bob the Manx had joined Jud and his guest. He lay on the bow thwart and watched alertly as the trout danced across the bottom of the boat.

Jud's hands were full of oars.

"Bob!" he said sharply. The big Manx cat instantly leaped from his perch onto the flopping fish, biting it once behind the head. Bob stood back. The fish vibrated for a second and went limp.

The Laughing Trout

Bob licked his forelegs and settled back onto his seat.
"Did you train him to do that?" asked the wide-eyed man.
"No. He just seems to read my mind."
"I'll be damned," said the guest.

CHAPTER TEN

Another Mystery

With Bob and the Seattle man in the truck, Mark began loading the boat onto its trailer. He saw Mark coming toward him, clipboard in hand.

"'Lo," said Mark cautiously but ever-smilingly.

"Hello, Mark. Interesting story in the *Post Register* this morning," said Jud.

"Yes. I thought so, too. Lemme check your fish," said Mark.

"No *Oncorhynchus bosham*," said Jud, biting his lip. "I already checked."

"I gotta check anyway," said Mark, lifting the cooler lid in the boat. He lifted the first fish and marked his sheet. He lifted the second fish.

"What's this?" said Mark, looking at Bob's bite punctures on the rainbow trout.

The Laughing Trout

"I don't know," said Jud, looking up at the cab of the truck. The plump man was listening to a baseball game through his earphones.

Why not? Jud thought mischievously. "That fish was fighting hard when he hooked him. When we got him in, he was real limp," said Jud, wiping the gunwales of the dory with a cloth.

Mark looked intently at the fish. "It's been bitten!"

"Looks that way," said Jud, polishing the brass fittings on the oarlock.

"It's been bitten by a vicious trout!" said Mark. "A victim of *Oncorhynchus bosham*!" he said excitedly. "I'll have to take the fish," said Mark, using his official voice.

"I'll tell my client," nodded Jud.

The truck bounced into Vera's.

"I owe you a drink, Mr. Denkers. Game biologist confiscated that last trout you caught. He wants to study it. Something peculiar about it," he said.

Mr. Denkers was pleasantly philosophical about helping advance the cause of wildlife biology.

Day Fourteen
Island Park

CHAPTER ELEVEN

A Fanged and Vicious Trout

Jud pulled his truck alongside Vera's van and the only other vehicle in Vera's parking lot: an old white Ford Fairlane four-door with twin spotlights and a large, whippy aerial still shimmying, indicating that Beal Finnegan, the Island Park marshal and mechanic, must have recently arrived. Jud yawned as the first rays of sun warmed his back.

He crunched through the gravel, clomped over the board porch and heard the familiar *gritch* of the door hinge as the smell of coffee and cooking oil greeted him from the doorway of Vera's Laughing Trout.

"'Lo, Vera. 'Lo, Beal," greeted Jud as he intercepted the steaming coffee cup Vera rumbled down the counter toward him.

"Mornin', Jud," said Beal Finnegan, whose pale blond eyebrows bobbed over blue eyes that blinked from beneath a Smokey Bear hat that he wore everywhere, year 'round. His jowls jiggled from the aftershock of the greeting.

The Laughing Trout

Don't you think it's time Island Park got a full-time marshal?" he asked Jud, obviously continuing a conversation that had been in swing before Jud sat down. "Full" sounded like "fool" from Beal's plump, tongue-licked lips.

Jud answered: "Why? You need more to do? Seems to me that between your Chevron station and convenience store and Finnegan Towing you'd have enough going on to drive you properly crazy."

"My old lady and kids take care of the station well enough durin' the busy time. With a fool-time marshal, Island Park could become solvent," Beal said, blinking directly at Jud, then turning as he heard Vera's voice.

"Beal Finnegan, you just like playing cop. My God, you let your kid change my blowout and he put on the wrong size tire," Vera reminded him. "You should be paying more attention to what you've got. You put my bug screen on backwards and I know you can read."

"Now wait a minute, I took care of the tire and, dammit, if you'd bring that van in I'd fix the boog screen. What I am talking about is raising the financial wherewithal of the township through a *conservation program*," he said with a sincere look, twisting uncomfortably in his twill pants.

Vera looked at Jud: "Beal says six moose were hit on Route 20 last year. Says if he became a full-time marshal, and if the township funded him a radar set, he could pass out speeding tickets."

"To the moose?" said Jud.

"Seriously, we could raise a lot of money through fines. Why there's lots of speeders come through every day," Beal said defensively.

"Bullshit, Beal," said Vera. "We'd get a bad reputation in no time at all. Folks would avoid Island Park. The people down in Rexburg even have a Route 20 Festival to promote travel along the road through here and to Yellowstone. God knows it's hard enough competing with the Interstate," she said, wiping the counter.

"You stick to patrolling the empty cabins and handling the rowdies on the weekends. You do a good job of keeping the college and high school kids in line; and when a serious malefactor makes his presence known, you call the Idaho State Police or the Forest Service Law Enforcement, like always," said Vera officially. Vera was a member of the community council and contributed $500 a year in cash and $500 a year in meals to Beal's $6,000 a year job.

"What about the moose?" said Beal.

"Life is risky for all of us, even the guy who hits the poor moose," said Vera sharply. "Drivers get a few moose, moose get a few drivers. It evens out, Beal," she said with a tone that meant she would hear no more of the subject.

"What'll you have for breakfast?" said Vera to Jud as she served sausage and eggs to the already working lips of the porcine marshal.

"T-bone steak, rare," Jud said, reaching for the newspaper as he sucked in his hot coffee noisily and gingerly.

"You want a salad with it?" Vera was no longer surprised at Jud's breakfast orders.

"Yep. Roquefort dressing," said Jud, stretching. He saw a new sign over Vera's kitchen:

The Floggings Will Continue Until Morale Improves

He smiled as he opened the paper. His smile faded as the headline leaped at him from the front page:

BIG REWARD OFFERED
FOR NEW IDAHO TROUT

The Laughing Trout

IDAHO FALLS (AP)—An Idaho fisheries biologist announced a reward of $50,000 for anyone catching and keeping alive the fanged trout recently discovered in the Henrys Fork of the Snake River near Island Park.

Mark Harvey Bosham said that he had been able to create a reward fund by asking private and public donors to pledge money for the capture.

The State of Idaho has pledged $5,000, with undisclosed additional amounts pledged by Trout Unlimited, The Fisheries Society, Theodore Gordon Flyfishers, QUEST FOR TROUT TV program, and Bone Dry Tackle Company.

Bosham announced discovery of two of the specimens of the new trout last week. Both were taken by fishermen. Neither was kept alive.

"We need a live specimen in order to take samples of living tissue so we can thoroughly investigate its genetics," said Bosham.

He also indicated that at least one rainbow trout caught by a fisherman on the river Monday had been attacked and killed by the vicious new species.

"The fisherman had hooked a nice rainbow when suddenly the trout leaped from the water, its fangs biting into the base of the head of the rainbow. It tailwalked, shaking the rainbow as a pit bull shakes a Pekinese," said Bosham, who claims to be the first to describe the fish for science.

"There's no doubt about it. The fang marks fit perfectly with the fangs of our two specimens," he added.

The reward is payable to the first fisherman who delivers a live "Bosham trout" to the game biologist in Island Park.

CHAPTER TWELVE

Keeping the Lid On

"Hi, Rollo. You hear about it?" said Jud, holding the static-sputtering phone away from his ear.

Instead of an angry or hurt Rollo Pasko, Jud heard a tinkle of laughter. "Oh yeah, we heard it about it," said Pasko. "The fisheries people are mildly curious, but they haven't put it together with my Lago Poopo work."

"Didn't they see the picture on the internet?" said Jud."

No. And the papers in D.C. didn't run a photo. Politics—not pisces—are what people are focused on here. The State Department people who fund us haven't made a peep. "'Course when the *Weekly World News* runs the picture and claims it's the progeny of an eight-year-old Italian schoolgirl, they may see it at the supermarket," chuckled Rollo. "No. I'm not in trouble—yet. But see if you can't put a lid on this. Did you play a practical joke?" 'Strange Trout Drives Fish Biologist Barking Mad.' Now that's a headline to your satisfaction!"

"I didn't expect it to go this far," said Jud.

"Then you underestimate the ego of your cousin. Just don't let anyone know where those fish came from," said Pasko. "I can see more headlines: Government Hires Mad Scientist to Alter Genes. Brrrrrr," he shuddered.

Day Fifteen
San Francisco

CHAPTER THIRTEEN

Enter Suzanne Hsu

Suzanne Hsu's spiked heels clicked sharply in the hallway as she approached the entry. A brass plaque next to the glass doors proclaimed: *National Broadcasting Corporation* She straightened her burgundy cravat against its silk blouse, smoothed the skirt of the blue-black suit, and pushed through the peacock-painted door.

John Albrecht, the gay receptionist, watched her stride past; she walked like a dancer, head up, on her toes. Whenever she came in, it struck him that she seemed too tall to be Asian. He admired her long, curvaceous legs with muscular calves. He wished he had legs like that.

"Hi, Suzanne," said the receptionist. Michael wants to see you as soon as you get in."

"Morning, Johnny," she said as she thumbed through her stack of mail. She picked up the bundle and continued scanning the envelopes as she walked through the busy studio.

The Laughing Trout

Suzanne pushed through the door marked: *Michael Goff, Managing Producer.*

"Morning, Michael. What's up?" she asked, as she slid into the Mies chair in front of his desk. She continued thumbing through her mail.

"Hi. No small talk, even?" said the tan, balding man with graying hair and excitable face. He undid the button on his navy blazer and smoothed his regimental-stripe tie as he looked at the woman.

Suzanne Hsu was going places. Audience response spiked up each time the network ran one of her stories. The word had come down that with a little more audience recognition, she'd go to New York or D.C. After that, maybe a morning host slot.

There were those who saw in Suzanne Hsu prime anchor material. For ten years after college, she had been an anchor in smaller markets: Santa Barbara, Spokane, Dayton. She got good marks for her research and journalistic aggression; she polished her presentation to showbiz sparkle.

Then the NBC affiliate in San Francisco hired her. She specialized in politics. A network feed of her story on bribes to legislators by California land developers caught the attention of NBC executives in New York. A month later she was hopping across the West covering the presidential campaign. Americans remembered her best for her comeback to the candidate when she said: "Sir, that is patent nonsense."

Now Michael Goff was certain the new network assignment for Suzanne Hsu was designed to give luster and to soften her diamond-hard, Asian brilliance. In a word, they liked her and wanted her to move up.

He looked at the lovely, uptilted face before him. A tropical sea of exotic beauty, he thought. The thick lashes swept across her green-brown eyes, and a light spray of fine freckles washed down either side of her small nose and faded as they rose to meet her high cheekbones. The spindrift of her curly black hair glistened in the morning light, forming a halo against the gold of her skin.

Her full mouth, slick and red as a dark cherry, beckoned to him sensually, recalling the one night when Suzanne might have truly loved him. Now he was not at all sure how she felt. She was away so much that there was no continuity to the relationship. He came around the desk and leaned down to kiss her on the cheek.

Suzanne was acutely aware of the man's feelings; he'd made it clear over the year she'd been working with him. Once, after dinner and much wine, there had been a moment of…was it need? Or was it weakness? Or was it merely the fact that Suzanne wanted more network assignments? She had not analyzed having sex with Michael and thought it best not to. Suzanne feared she might not like her motives.

Today she had a lot on her mind. There was an early story to cover.

"I don't mean to be brusque," she said. She smiled and tilted her head to one side. "I've got to be in Sacramento by 11:00 for the governor's conference." She continued thumbing through the mail.

"Okay. Small talk later? Over dinner?"

"Maybe. What's up?"

"Did you read the piece in the *Chronicle* yesterday on that weird trout in a place called Island Park in Idaho?" asked Michael.

"I saw it on their website. It's an odd story," said Suzanne, looking up.

"New York called yesterday afternoon. They asked if I thought you should cover it. I saw that it would present to

The Laughing Trout

the public another side of Suzanne Hsu, so naturally I said I'd ask you," Michael added.

"Michael, this could be *it!*" For the moment everything else was forgotten. She jumped from the chair and kissed him.

He smiled wanly. Perhaps this would help her realize why it was important to love him.

"And where is Island Park?" asked Suzanne.

"About here," said Michael. He noisily unfolded a map and put his finger on a point where Idaho, Wyoming, and Montana came together.

"It's roughly between Idaho Falls, here, and West Yellowstone." The map indicated mostly forest lands. There was a small blip marked *Island Park*, a wandering blue wiggle titled *Henry's Fork, Snake R.*, and a fish-shaped blue spot named *Island Park Reservoir.*

"It looks like it's a million miles from nowhere. How do I get there?"

"Fly to Salt Lake, then pick up a flight to West Yellowstone. Rent a car. A web search brings up a place called the 'Laughing Trout Bar and Motel' at a village called Last Chance. Here's the number. "It may be *very* rustic, however." Your crew will be Dexter and Pelligrini. They won't get in until Friday. They're in Florida covering the NASA spectacular," he added.

"I've worked with Dexter. I want to leave in the morning so I can get backgrounded," said Suzanne Hsu.

"Dinner tonight?"

"Sorry, Michael," she said, gently laying her hand on his sleeve. "I have to do some research so I can keep an appointment with an ugly fish."

Day Fifteen
West Yellowstone

CHAPTER FOURTEEN

A Nature Boy

Christopher Gurney Cochran fingered his long, matted hair and rubbed the paper coffee cup across the bars of the West Yellowstone city jail. In an earlier time it would have been tin instead of paper and would have made a rattle satisfactory enough to summon the jailer.

Since the spider fight, he had had the cell to himself, which was some consolation. His former cellmate, a Livingston mechanic with short dark hair, a full beard and steel-blue eyes, serving fifteen days for shoplifting a wrench set and a carton of malted milk balls, had killed a spider which had webbed itself a home in a corner. The enraged six-foot Cochran, brown eyes blazing with fury, clouted the mechanic to the floor with a quick chop of his right fist.

Fortunately the other cell in the jail had been emptied of a disorderly cowboy, and the mechanic was removed to it for his own safety.

The Laughing Trout

As it was, Cochran's coffee was now gone, his oatmeal finished, and for each of the thirty days he had been here he knew that the next offering would be the Idaho Falls *Post Register*, once the jailer finished reading it. He paced now, humming "If I Had the Wings of an Angel," looking down at the worn leather of his big, round-toed hiking boots. He looked for the billionth time at the single caged light that glared down from the ceiling: it was right to dynamite nine U.S. Forest Service trail signs, even if the last blast had thrown him to the ground and left him partly deaf. He'd cut the fuse too short.

It was proper that he had come forth to take responsibility for the blasts. Why act like a typical human who dodged responsibility, who tried to blame other persons, creatures ,and circumstances for their own problems, and then like a jackal, shit and sneaked away?

Cochran paused to considered the human-jackal simile: Jackals were jackals, doing jackal things, like scavenging to survive, a useful contribution to earth's harmony. Humans were aberrations, committing acts of violence and acquisition for no reason but ego—excessive, materialistic, out of control, bringing death, filth, and noise, and defiling beauty in the name of progress. The simile was not fair to jackals, he decided.

The youth's philosophy tussled in conflict in the depths of Cochran's very soul: He was convinced that violent acts against man's *property* were a necessary counterbalance to the crimes being committed against nature by humankind. But could he justify causing physical pain, even in disgusting living human things? They were after all, creatures of the earth, too.

Or did man deserve harsher retribution for the pain he inflicted on the earth's other living things?

A Nature Boy

Among his youthful group of practitioners of eco-sabotage, the controversy had been a major campfire subject as they furtively spiked four-wheel drive trails and sugared the gas tanks of wilderness road construction equipment. Poison a sheep? Spike a redwood tree?

Christopher Cochran would never knowingly commit an act that would hurt an animal or even a human. And yes, he would be publicly responsible for his actions. He could live with that.

Acknowledging his responsibility for the sign blasts, Christopher Cochran had marched into the local newspaper.

"Mea culpa," he told a reporter.

"You a culpa," said the judge, and gave him thirty days in the West Yellowstone jail, and two years suspended with a fine of $1,975 to replace the signs.

Cochran was at first proud of joining the ranks of Gandhi and King in civil disobedience.

Now he was sick of the white walls, black bars, and gray food. He was glad that at noon his time was done. Christopher Gurney Cochran, at twenty, was already an ex-convict. He had served a thirty-day term the year before when he was sentenced for malicious interference in Nevada.

He had telephoned the county sheriff and announced that a baby was lost in an area the Bureau of Land Management was to begin chaining that day. Chaining is a process whereby the pinion, juniper, and sage are ripped from the earth by a massive iron chain pulled between two bulldozers, a practice alleged to produce better range for cattle.

"I didn't say what kind of baby, your honor," Christopher told the Nevada judge at the preliminary hearing.

"Baby rabbits, baby birds, baby snakes. They all live there," he said.

The Laughing Trout

Now the wizened, white-haired West Yellowstone jailer, so slight that he looked lopsided from the heavy ring of keys on his right hip, shuffled to Christopher's cell.

He could hear the boy singing.

"You want this today, St. Vitus?" he said, his voice aquiver as he proffered the daily newspaper. The old man had come to like the "hippie" with the tangled hair and cheeks fiery with acne. Occasionally the boy became almost electrically charged with strange ideas.

The kid couldn't sit still. Saint Vitus Dance, they called it when the jailer was a boy. The nickname suited the youth, the old man thought.

"What's that?" said Cochran, jerked away from his basso rendition of "Stormy Monday", cupping his hand behind his ever-ringing ear.

"Oh, thank you, Evan," said Christopher to the old jailer, taking the paper through the bars.

"I bet you're through exploding signs, aren't you?" said the jailer, looking over his half-spectacles.

"I'd go out and do it again this afternoon, if need be," Christopher said levelly. "Man makes a mess of nature wherever he goes. My mission is to make certain—through any means—that man finally is made to recognize how he abuses Mother Earth. If my acts are what it takes to make man realize that he is responsible, then I will gladly defend nature again and again."

"Wheee-ew. St. Vitus, you talk like a politician," grumbled the jailer.

"Nope. Justice is all I want. Justice for all—just like in the pledge of allegiance. 'With liberty and justice for all,' and that means *all creatures*."

"Yep," said the jailer, scratching his thinning white hair.

A Nature Boy

"Politician all right. Politician in the year 2025. Thank God, I'll be gone by then," he said, shaking his head. "Man will have et his last pork chop 'cause the politicians will have outlawed killin' hogs," he muttered, shuffling back to the desk.

Christopher Cochran settled back with the newspaper. The story of the strange trout instantly caught his eye. The Island Park-West Yellowstone country was his newly adopted home and he was prickly-alert to the nuances of the tale. A $50,000 reward would have one certain effect: people would pour in, pounding the place to pulp. They would pee in the creeks, leave diapers strewn through the campgrounds, and drive madly through all the fragile meadows to reach fishing spots. That old English satirist, what was his name? He had the right idea, he thought: the solution to the problem is to eat babies. Human babies. *Ergo*, solution to famine as well as problems of human commercial-political expansionism. His college professor-parents in Michigan might muster a wan smile for the premise and realize he was just kidding.

In the meantime, he would do something. The situation compelled action. Human pollution threatened his beautiful Snake River. "*I'm a little red rooster*," he sang softly as he planned his next coup.

CHAPTER FIFTEEN

The Sufferings of H.H. Sponzini

Herbert Hoover Sponzini's chest heaved gently as the doctor placed the cold stethoscope on his left nipple. Sponzini longed for the more familiar surroundings of a military medical facility. The infirmary at Lyndon B. Johnson Space Center always felt more comfortable to the retired officer, and the specialist here at Jefferson Davis Hospital in downtown Houston was expensive, efficient, obnoxious, and mouthy.

During his last tour of duty—teaching ROTC at the University of Houston—Sponzini was ordered to report for his annual physical. A few aches and pains, he told the doctor as he stood ramrod straight, then turned his head and coughed. It came as a decided shock when the medical diagnosis was different. Sponzini always told the doctors his lower back pains were doubtless caused by his old Vietnam War wound. (He'd been shot in the ass while unloading equipment at DaNang. Accidentally. By one of his own men). This time the back pain seemed to extend to his lower legs. Dangerous blood clots, said the medicos at LBJ, referring him to this young Dr. Zimmerman, a specialist who had an insolence Sponzini detested.

"You know why turds are tapered, Colonel?" asked Dr. Zimmerman.

Sponzini stopped breathing for a moment, then he thought better of responding.

"So your ass won't slam shut, haw haw," said the boisterous doctor.

Sponzini said nothing, stoically looking past the hairy ear of the examining doctor. After all his years in the Army, he still found crudeness distasteful. His upbringing in a strict Catholic home in Ohio had impressed on young Sponzini the need for modesty and purity of mind. Thank God, I was an officer, he thought.

Sometimes he regretted never having married, but even now the thought of all that personal *exposure* to another individual caused discomfort. He early-on became inured to his widowed mother's endless carping about his bachelorhood and had cocooned his guilt in military dedication.

As he looked down, he saw his stomach pooching out like a melon. He sucked it in self-consciously, as if standing before one of his ROTC classes. He sighed at the fat that marbled his chest and stomach, having taken over his torso in the year since the clots had limited his physical activities.

"Well, Gomer, you're gonna survive," said Dr. Zimmerman rising, a twinkle in his eye.

"I fought wars for your kind, doctor. I'll thank you to call me 'colonel'," Sponzini said stuffily.

The Sufferings of H.H. Sponzini

"Whoa! That ol' war wound must have maimed your sense of humor. I meant no offense, Colonel," said Zimmerman levelly.

Sponzini sulked.

"Colonel, the clots seemed to have dissipated. As long as you remain on the Teperzine you can go about your normal life," said Zimmerman, marking the colonel's chart. "I want you to ease into activities. Light exercise only. And you know about the medication?"

"Yes," said Sponzini. "But I plan to go fishing. Okay?"

"From a boat or wading?," asked the doctor "From a boat," said Sponzini.

"Sure. Just take it easy and don't get chilled or cold or there can be side effects from Teperzine. You understand?"

Of course I understand, you boob, thought Sponzini, buttoning his shirt as the doctor left the room.

He looked forward with excitement to his trip.

There was still much planning and checklisting and preparing, he realized, hurrying from the hospital.

Day Fifteen
Salt Lake City

CHAPTER SIX TEEN

Enter Frieda and Rulon Cox

Frieda Cox smoothed her print dress over her fat legs. She wheezed as she caught her breath, the walk from the kitchen having provided her with a day's aerobics.

"Now. What was you trying to read to me?" she asked her husband, her broad, placid face looking down on the little man as she offered a plate of warm cookies.

Rulon ("Cuss") Cox adjusted his suspenders, then snapped the paper to upright stiffness. He took a cookie but did not bite into it.

"It says: 'a $50,000 dollar reward has been offered to the person providing a live specimen of this trout.'"

Frieda was very interested in this story. She ate five cookies while listening intently. With her bald, hook-nosed fishing partner and husband of forty years, she had often fished in Island Park. Fishing had become their lives, now that his railroad retirement had allowed time. Mostly they fished lakes and reservoirs these days—all over the West, and any time of year. Nothing suited Frieda better than the hum of tires on the highway, followed by the gentle wash of waves on a pebble beach.

And there was now more money than Frieda ever dreamed of. Rulon, always a secretive skinflint, had painfully revealed to his wife just how much he had in his accounts and funds.

It would still have been a secret if Rulon had not gotten sick on the Easter ham. He thought he was dying.

As the pain of demise ate into his bowels, he spewed up everything, including his secret accounts and the amount of his pension fund. He thought the calm that ensued was the serenity that came just before death, but to his surprise he was mostly better the next day.

A stunned Frieda marched a recovered Rulon through the local Sears store on an appliance-buying binge and then turned her attention to the serious business of re-outfitting for fishing.

As Frieda gripped him by his symbolic ear, Rulon bought a new Dodge pickup truck, a new camper (complete with real wood cupboards and closets, shower and TV), a new eighteen-foot aluminum boat and a 45-horsepower outboard motor.

Other women might have wanted jewelry and trips to Hawaii; Frieda liked being encapsulated in her homey camper with chintz curtains and the heavy fragrance of frying fish. She even concocted a recipe for her favorite dish: Trout-aroni, a combination of noodles and trout in a dill cream sauce.

"If we caught that fish, we could replace all this money you've made me spend," grumbled Rulon. He ruminated for a while."Makes sense to me that the fish they are after may have come out of Island Park Reservoir to spawn in the river," he said.

"Let's go," said Frieda, her voice muffled by cookies. "Let's go." She jiggled in her chair at the thought and found room in an unoccupied alcove of her mouth for yet another oatmeal sandy.

Day Fifteen
Rexburg, Idaho

CHAPTER SEVEN TEEN

Two Locals

Forty miles south of Last Chance, where the Snake River spread acres of rich soil across the flat plain, lonely gravel roads grid the vast potato and grain farms. A few trees spring up as windbreaks.

Gordon Okleberry bounced gently in the seat of the air-conditioned John Deere. Over the stereo headset, he was hearing a song, "Baby's Got Her Blue Jeans On." With the rocking of the tractor on his balls and the sound of music in his ears, his thoughts were on sex instead of on his 2,000 acre farm and its myriad activities of early summer. Maybe his wife would let him do it to her again.

He watched a pair of meadow larks copulating on the fence wire. At the end of the row, standing next to a car glinting in the wavy noon heat, in a green sports coat and tie, stood Max Dodick, a smile on his eager face, waving his arms to attract Okleberry's attention.

The Laughing Trout

Dodick was vice president of sales for Ut-Ida Implement, the John Deere dealer in Idaho Falls. Okleberry was one of his customers—and a life-long friend. He was also a neighbor, living only a few miles away.

Okleberry finished spraying the row and shut off the tractor. He swung down from the cab.

"'Lo, Max," he said with a agreeable smile, pushing the baseball cap back on his graying brown hair.

"'Lo, Gordon," said the tall snag-faced implement salesman.

"Something special bring you out?"

"I was hopin' you'd wanna break for lunch," said Dodick, squinting in the midday sun. He lifted a big hand to shade his eyes.

Gordon Okleberry licked his dry lips. He adjusted his overall straps and rubbed his double chin.

"Don't think I'd better chance it. Judy is still pissed-off from last time we went to lunch."

"'Cause you were so drunk?" said Dodick.

"'Cause I didn't get home for two days," said Okleberry.

They both scuffed thoughtfully at the black, Snake River soil.

"Judy thinks you and I together are like matches and gasoline," said Okleberry, smiling, but not looking at Dodick.

"Yeah. The women get so they don't trust you anymore. I mean, hell, it's not like we do it but once in a while. 'S always been that way, since we was in high school," Dodick said, puzzled.

"Yeah. Man's got to let off steam now and then. Judy thinks it went too far last time," said Okleberry.

"She didn't appreciate the gift you brought back from Salt Lake?" Dodick giggled.

"Hell, that was an expensive shotgun," said Okleberry indignantly.

74

Two Locals

They were silent for a moment.

"Maybe we ought to go fishin'," said Dodick. "Then we can whoop and holler all we want."

"'at's a thought," said Okleberry cheerily. They were silent again. "Couldn't go too long this time of year. We'd have to go close by."

"Hell, go up to Island Park. Did you see that trout they found up there?" said Dodick.

"Odd, wasn't it," said Okleberry, nodding.

"Let's go catch one. Nobody is better'n us on the Snake. You 'n me been fishing Henry's Fork since we were five and there's a fifty thousand dollar reward for it if it's caught alive," said Dodick, scratching his neck. You could buy Judy a better shotgun this time." He burst into laughter.

They were quiet again.

"I do need a break," said the plump-faced farmer, looking across the vast rows of fresh-up potatoes. He had been working seven days a week since March. The farm wouldn't miss him for a long weekend.

"Let's do it. But we gotta make a pact that we won't get crazy. Judy ain't gonna like it, no matter what," said Okleberry with a sigh, licking his sun-dried lips in anticipation.

"Oh, Bev'll grit her teeth all weekend. But we can show them they can trust us. Yeah. We'll make a pact not to get crazy," said Dodick.

They shook hands.

Dodick looked thoughtful for a moment, then spoke: "I've got a sales call in Ashton Saturday morning. I'll just take all my stuff and meet you there. We can leave one car there, then leave after a leisurely lunch at the VFW Club." He rubbed his hands at the thought.

"See you Saturday," said Okleberry as he climbed onto his tractor.

Day Sixteen
Island Park

CHAPTER EIGHTEEN

A Wee Clash

"Hello, Mr. Buckalew?" The woman's voice was rich and confident. "My name is Suzanne Hsu and I want to hire your services for tomorrow and Sunday."

Jud interrupted her.

"Ma'am, I am booked both tomorrow and Sunday. There's been a reward offered for an alleged trout and I am scheduled full."

This was Jud's fifth call of the morning. Maybe fishermen were not really expecting to catch the Lago Poopo trout and get the reward, thought Jud, but it sure seemed that the *possibility* helped the bookings. It was like a goddamn lottery, he thought.

"But you don't understand. I am Suzanne Hsu. With NBC News."

"Well, congratulations. I am Jud Buckalew and I'm still booked."

The Laughing Trout

Suzanne Hsu was coming to the realization that she had connected with a man who did not know who she was.

"NBC *television*," she emphasized. Better pour it on, Suzanne thought. She had taken a cabin at Vera's Laughing Trout and had instantly wowed Vera Segura, an inveterate television watcher. Not many celebrities came to Island Park.

A little compliment to frost the cake: "Vera Segura said you are the best guide on the river. We're going to be doing a story on the search for this fish, and we want you to carry me and the crew. We'll be using footage of you and your boat on national television. Wouldn't you like to see yourself on TV?"

"I do not own a television set. I am booked tomorrow and Sunday. If you want a story about Bosham's trout, talk to Bosham," said Jud, the irritation rising in his voice.

"I already have. I am meeting with him today. He's really going out of his way for us, Mr. Buckalew."

Jud lost it.

"Mark would suck a duck's butt if he thought it would do him any good. Lady, I am booked. That's that," he said angrily.

"Look, we'll double your fee."

She heard the receiver click and then the steady hum the dial tone.

"I'll be damned," she said. She really wanted this Buckalew fellow. Vera Segura said he'd been guiding the boat that caught the first fish. And snapshots at Vera's of Buckalew with his fish and fishermen showed him to be tall, craggy, photogenic—a real forest ranger type, except for the anomalous aviator's dark glasses.

Day Seventeen
Island Park

CHAPTER NINETEEN

A Good Fight and A Good Dance Make A Satisfactory Idaho Soiree

"One more Saturday night, hey ya' little Saturday night," sang an off-key Jud Buckalew as he shaved in the mirror. Bob rubbed against his wet ankles, as Manx cats do to renew the oil in their pelts. He pulled his best burgundy wool Pendleton shirt over a yellow turtleneck and stuffed the ensemble into faded jeans. He tugged the Justin boots from their trees and dusted them with his socks. With his boots on, Jud turned back to the mirror, splashed his cheeks with aftershave, and took one last swipe with a comb.

"Hello, Darlin'," he said, winking at the face in the mirror.

Saturday night in Island Park. It was dark when Buckalew pulled up to the Laughing Trout. Rows of cars and trucks lined the parking lot and flowed in parallel lines down Route

The Laughing Trout

20. Smoke curled from the chimney and hung in strata in the branches of the pines. Neon beer signs beckoned cheerily. Music inside the lodge made the windows vibrate and shimmy. The door of the bar glowed brightly; a rush of warm air from the door spilled the promise of grilling steaks and whiskey into the cool evening.

"VERA!" Jud howled as he stepped through the door. "WHERE THE HELL ARE YA?" Every head in the place snapped around.

"I'M READY, JUDDY" shouted Vera as she took off her apron and headed from the kitchen.

The local regulars applauded. When Buckalew danced with Segura, it was the official signal to begin Saturday night at Last Chance. And if there was one thing Jud Buckalew was good at besides fishing, it was dancing. The band, farm boys from Ashton and St. Anthony, smashed into what sounded like "Why Do Fools Fall in Love?" Jud and Vera wiggled and jumped and bopped and glided until they were the only ones on the floor. Vera moved sensually and slow at times, then wildly tossed her head and flared her skirt as Jud did a little shuffle and a split. Snap! A spin as Jud tossed off Vera toward the nearest booths, catching her deftly and spinning her back into his arms.

The band broke into "Green Onions." Jud and Vera circled each other slowly, down low, pelvises cocked and lethal, arcing a leg, moving an arm up and then lowering it slowly, synchronizing perfectly. The packed house applauded when they wrapped it up with an Idaho fandango to "Sharp Dressed Man." Jud slumped into a chair. Emmy, the Saturday night waitress, came by with her dollars folded between her fingers.

"Club soda with a twist," said Jud, panting. He began to look around the darkened lodge as he caught his breath.

A Good Fight and A Good Dance Make A Satisfactory Idaho Soiree

The booths were packed. The tables had been pushed back from the pinewood dance floor. Cowboys from the Snake River Plain, a few timbermen in huge, round-toed boots, and knots of dude fishermen sat drinking, eating and boisterously laughing, nearly drowned-out by the sound of the band.

Jud began to look for women. They trickled in shyly from the cabins and summer homes and lodges and farms in the area—high school and college girls, career women on vacation, divorcees and restless wives on the make.

His gaze rested on a booth near the fire. "My, oh my," he said aloud as he saw the woman with the arching eyebrows, creamy tan skin and tousled black hair. She was looking at him.

Jud ordinarily might have walked over to her, introduced himself, and moved in. But this woman was extraordinary. An kind of oriental mirage. A beauty so luscious that it clenched at his guts—an unreachable, impossible beauty that made him shy.

And then, to his astonishment, the man sitting with her stood up to reveal himself as Mark Harvey Bosham, complete with billowing white pipe and ever-moving lips fixed in an endless grin.

Byrrh!" shouted Mark. "B-Y-R-R-H," he spelled it loudly.

"Why's he keep yelling beer?" said Vera as she passed Jud.

"His way of showing he's sophisticated," said Jud. "He's drunk enough to think he's Ernest Hemingway. Byrrh is a some kind of French drink."

"He was doin' that with them school teachers.""The ubiquitous Mark," muttered Jud Buckalew to himself as he slumped in the chair and took a sip of club soda. His mood fell. He absently acknowledged the calls and hellos of friends as they passed the table. He shook hands with his fisherman

The Laughing Trout

of that day and exchanged a few words about the current hatch. Jud could not take his eyes off the woman.

The din grew as more people arrived and the band amped-up. Drunks argued volubly. Dancers dripped with sweat. Pencils drew lines on napkins as heads bowed in instructional reverence.

Jud desperately wanted to ask the woman to dance.

Inside him a struggle raged: dread of rejection versus fear of success.

He closed his eyes and took a deep breath. *Hey, I'm a good guy.* With these words of self-affirmation, he stood and headed for the booth where the woman and Mark sat.

"Would you like to dance?" he blurted out, over the sound of the band. She looked up at him. A hint of a smile spread her across her cupid's-bow lips. She slid from the booth and Jud nearly melted. She had a figure to match the face. The first thing he noticed was that her shoulders were broader than her hips. She had long legs, sheathed in tight jeans. A concho belt hung in a swag off one hip. Her ivory silk blouse caught the sheen of the firelight.

She put her hand up. He took it. They swirled away on the dance floor, pummeled by the beat of the band and the throb of the crowd. Mark Bosham chuffed suavely on his pipe, looking obliviously up at the wall.

"My name is Jud," he said loudly, close to her ear so he could be heard over the band.

"Mine's Suzanne," she said, pulling back and looking up at him. "Where did you learn to dance? You're good."

"The winters are long and cold in Paris, Idaho. I practiced for hours alone in my basement when I was growing up," he shouted.

A Good Fight and A Good Dance Make A Satisfactory Idaho Soiree

"Paris, *Idaho?*" She paused, pushing him away. "I think I was being put-on by my host," she said, nodding toward Bosham.

"Put-on is putting it mildly," Jud nodded. So far, so good. A warning shot across Mark's bows could slow the bullshit. Women were one area where Jud could always best his cousin. Always had, always would. Mark had no patience, no sense of development. It never ceased to amaze Jud that Mark would attempt such nonsense. Ah well: he had heard what they said about a roomful of chimps striking at typewriter keys. Sooner or later, odds were that one would write a beautiful sonnet. Maybe that was Mark's strategy with women. Hit on all of 'em.

"Where are you from?" Jud's confidence was returning.

"San Francisco," she said.

"I haven't seen you around before," Jud said, whirling her under his arm, then deftly pulling her in close.

"We met on the phone yesterday," she said.

He slowed and held her at arms length again. "Yesterday?"

"Yesterday. I'm Suzanne Hsu. With NBC. Remember?"

"Oh, God." Jud came to a halt. He gulped.

Confidence was ebbing fast.

"I guess I was abrupt on the phone. I apologize. I just can't cancel on customers or they don't come back. I should have explained that," said Buckalew.

"It would have helped," said Suzanne.

"On the other hand, you can't come in and play big shot like that and expect anything else," said Jud, strangely emboldened.

"In my business I do what works. 'NBC' and 'television' are magic words to most folks," she said, looking up at Jud.

"I guess it didn't work this time," said Jud.

"Look," she said, pulling away. "I'm just trying to do a job. You're trying to do a job. Leave it at that," she said, clearly seeking to end the conversation, her green-brown eyes sparkling with edginess.

She had spent the better part of two days with a motor-mouthed, egotistical Mark Bosham. Her camera crew had been shunted from Canaveral to Wichita to cover a tornado and they would not be in for at least another twenty-four hours. She was bored, burned out on two days of pine trees, ranch food, and rudimentary lodgings. She was being bombarded by noise and smoke.

Jud followed her helplessly back to the table, trying to think of something to say. She left his side without a word.

"I'm going to turn in," she said to Bosham.

"I'll walk you to your cabin," Bosham said loudly. Jud hung back, still strangling on his tongue. It was like trying to awaken from a bad dream. Not a word would come.

Fate hinges on strange circumstances. As Suzanne Hsu was about to turn, a voice from the next booth shouted out:"IT'S THE TV CHINK!"

The voice belonged to one Gordon Okleberry, Rexburg farmer and drinker of margaritas since noon of that day, when he and Max Dodick launched their sally against Henry's Fork trout from the VFW Club in Ashton. He was pointing at Suzanne Hsu.

Events turned quickly. Mark Bosham shrank back into the booth. Max Dodick tried to clap a hand over the farmer's shouting mouth. Okleberry bit down hard on Dodick's finger and Dodick flung his hand back, hitting a logger in the back of the head, knocking him forward into his beer.

"THAT'S NO WAY TO TALK TO THE LADY!" bellowed an angry Jud Buckalew, ending his aphasia impressively.

Jud stepped forward as the logger swung at Dodick.

A Good Fight and A Good Dance Make A Satisfactory Idaho Soiree

The big fist cracked into Jud's chin. He heard the band playing "Proud Mary." Jud watched the floor come up to meet him, then all was quiet.

Day Eighteeen
Island Park

CHAPTER TWENTY

Rapprochement

This day was too long, Jud thought as he leaned back in the chair on the porch of his cabin and watched the sun drop below the pines across the river. His head still ached from the punch the logger had thrown last night. He'd been out cold for ten minutes before coming to on the sofa in Vera's living room. His jaw was sore. His clients today had been demanding.

Too long. He felt too tired to fix dinner. He sipped a tall glass of iced coffee sweetened with cream and sugar.

Bob stalked mice in the wild flowers next to the porch, arching his back in preparation for a pounce. Then the cat suddenly relaxed and flattened out, settling deep into the blue lupine. Someone was coming down the trail.

In a moment Suzanne Hsu appeared, picking her way down the path with her arms outstretched for balance.

Jud stood up.

"Hi," she said softly as she halted at the foot of the steps.

The Laughing Trout

"Well, hello," said Jud, pulling his earlobe nervously.

"It's very pretty here," she said as she looked at the wild flowers and the river reflecting black and green and gold.

"Fills *me* up," said Jud. He struggled to find more words.

"I stopped by to thank you for last night," said Suzanne Hsu with warm eyes.

"To thank me? Wasn't my best night ever, I'll tell you," said Jud, feeling his jaw.

Her laughter was deep and burnished.

"You think it was funny?" he said.

"Yes. It was like a scene from a Three Stooges movie. The logger was so sorry he smacked you. He fell all over himself trying to be solicitous as they hauled you into what's-her-name's living room." She laughed in basso.

"What *wasn't* funny was the fool who shouted and caused the problem. I appreciate your defense of my honor and ancestry. That's why I came here," she said.

"Glad I tried to help—I guess," he said, rubbing his chin. Jud smiled shyly. He was beginning to feel at a loss for words again.

"Most men would not have done that. There seems to be too much risk involved to speak out on principle these days," she said, looking up at Jud on the porch through her heavy lashes. "Anyway, thanks." She nodded her head and turned to go.

Something in Jud was saying *Be brave.*

"Say, did you get your footage shot?" he blurted. She turned.

"The crew doesn't even get in until tomorrow morning. I can only find one guide and boat available tomorrow. We need two boats. One for the camera crew. This crazy fish business has people pouring in. They've hired all the guides," she said, shaking her head.

Rapprochement

Jud watched her shiny black hair bounce in the evening light. "You never asked me about Monday—tomorrow," he heard himself say mildly.

"You're available tomorrow?"

"I am."

"Mr. Buckalew, you are the answer to my prayers," said Suzanne Hsu, taking a deep breath.

"I'm really glad I can do it. Let's talk about what you are going to need. Would you like some iced coffee?" said Jud, holding up his glass.

She smiled as she saw it. "Looks more like a milkshake to me. And yes, I would."

"Well, come on up," said Jud. He held out his hand. He felt her cool fingers as he led her up the stairs to the porch.

"Wait one," he said, dashing into the cabin. In a moment he returned, dragging the rocker onto the porch.

"Just for guests," he said. "How do you like your iced coffee?"

"Black with sugar," she said, savoring the comfort of the rocker and the beauty of the view that lay before her.

Bob pushed against her leg. She reached down and felt the crackle of electricity as she stroked him. His purr was thunderous. Slowly she relaxed. For the first time in three days she felt comfortable on the Snake River.

"Are you originally from San Francisco?" asked Jud as he handed her a glass and napkin.

"No. Seattle was home. Born and raised there."

"College?"

"University of Washington."

"Did you study to be a TV star? Like, did you study broadcasting?"

She blushed and smiled. "No," said Suzanne Hsu. "I was a dance major, actually."

That explained her graceful walk to Jud.

"Hey, I'm the interviewer," said Suzanne. "Now, who are you?"

Jud told her of growing up in Paris, Idaho, and of college at Utah State.

"And why is it you detest your cousin?" she asked."

"I don't trust him," said Jud gloomily.

"Why?"

"Too long a story to bother with," he said, rising abruptly from his chair. "Look at that." He pointed to an osprey circling over the river. "An osprey. Hunting fish for his young. His nest is over on the edge of Island Park Reservoir." Jud watched the bird circle in purple-gold twilight. It hovered over the river flapping its hinged wings, then plunged into the river in a spatter of water. It splashed frantically, trying to become airborne.

"It's got a fish too big to lift," said Jud, glad to change the subject.

They watched in silence until at last the bird's struggle ended as the fish pulled free. The black and white bird rose and again began its circling.

"I think I know how he feels," Suzanne murmured.

"How's that?" said Jud.

"My work. I may have bitten off more than I can chew," she said, laughing lightly.

"Fame and money. Isn't that what it's all about?" Jud sipped his coffee.

"So they say. The best in my business seem to be motivated by that. I'm not sure that's what I want. But it looks like that's what I'm getting, and most people would be thrilled. But my father always said: 'If a man in the morning heads the right way, he may die in the evening without regret.' I am not sure if the way I am headed is the right way," she said, watching the osprey drift off.

Rapprochement

"Some folks are never certain of what they want. What would you do if you weren't doing this?" asked Jud.

"I would find a lovely place by the sea and teach children to dance," she said, sipping her coffee."

"Nice."

"I guess I better go find dinner," said Suzanne, rising.

"I haven't eaten myself, and we haven't discussed tomorrow's trip," said Jud. "Could I interest you in something simple—like steak and a salad?"

"No more steaks. That's all everybody seems to eat up here," she said.

Jud smiled serenely. Now he was on comfortable turf. He was used to catering to dude appetites.

"I happen to be a noted preparator of killer salads. Spinach, radishes, a little shredded carrot, some white asparagus, tomatoes, fresh mushrooms. Top it with my olive oil and lemon-vinegar dressing—heavy on the garlic—and *voila*. I happen to have buttery chunk of Havarti and some raw almonds to accompany it. Dessert: a humble but crisp apple."

"I'm sold," she said with smile. It sounded wonderful after three days of Vera's ranch-hand fare.

As Jud fixed the salad, Suzanne chattered about her career and how she had her first break reading weather reports on the cable weather channel. Then came an offer from a small market. Then another larger market. Finally, NBC.

"Where do you think you'll be in five years?" asked Jud as he set the heaping salad bowls on the placemats.

"I guess I want to be a network anchor," she said slowly and softly, hesitatingly.

"I hear that uncertainty again."

"Well, it's the top. The best you can do in my profession. My father taught me to strive to be the very best. To do otherwise was to demean yourself and your ancestors. I try to do the very best I can on every story I cover. I owe that to myself first of all. Without that integrity, I have nothing. Otherwise, I'm just another pretty television face. TV has enough of that."

She was silent for a moment, then asked. "How about you? What gives you the satisfaction of your career?"

"Being outdoors. It isn't the people. I don't really deal with people well. They make me uncomfortable. But being out here I see this marvelous, living world. There's a theory of the Earth as a living organism: the *Gaia* theory, it's called. Nature is mystical, endlessly changing, renewing, powering this dynamic system of life and death." He was quiet for a moment.

"Sometimes I can hear Gaia breathing. At sun-up she hums like electricity," he said. "Throw in the fragrance of pines and the sound of the river rolling by.

It's magic, spiritual. It cleanses me.

"Also, if I observe well I learn something new every day. Either about people, or critters. That's what makes my business okay," Jud added thoughtfully.

"They say you're the best on the river. Even your cousin says it," Suzanne remarked.

Jud was jerked back from his reverie.

"Praise from Caesar is praise indeed," he said. He was quiet a minute. "There was a time when everything I did was half-assed. Like you say, you only have your integrity. Here I can live simply and work on healing myself."

"Healing yourself?"

"Yeah, some of my past tore big chunks out of me."

"Tell me about that," she said in low, deep tones."

"I don't even know you," said Jud. He smiled to temper his words. Suzanne could see his fine, even teeth in the darkness of the porch.

Rapprochement

"You're right. I'm not doing a news interview. Sorry if I intruded on personal space," she said as she rose.

"It's late. I'd like to be on the river by 8:00 a.m. so we can have good light. I've been noticing the sun doesn't clear the pines until just after 8:00," she said. "Besides, I've got to see if my crew is in yet."

"Eight it is, then," agreed Jud. "We'll have to meet for breakfast and orientation at Vera's at 7:00. Bring some warm clothes 'cause you never know if the weather will turn. I'll walk you to your cabin," Jud said, reaching for the flashlight.

When Jud returned to his cabin, he could still smell her perfume and feel the touch of her hand on his arm.

He climbed into his bed. Bob curled up at his side.

"Thanks, Jud. It's been a lovely evening."

The words boomed in his head. It took a while for him to fall asleep.

CHAPTER TWENTY-ONE

Jud's Story

"Okay, people, here's the plan," said Suzanne Hsu as the group of five huddled over breakfast at Vera's.

She spoke with official producer demeanor.

Lulu Dexter, the diminutive blonde sound operator, and Don Pellegrini, the bearded, black-haired cameraman, stifled yawns. Suzanne looked at them sharply, a teacher's look of reproach for inattention.

"We hear ya, Suzanne. We are now in our ninth consecutive day of work and travel," said Pellegrini, eyes shut with resignation.

"I feel like I've been fuckin' gang-banged," huffed Lulu.

A startled Peter Pugmire, the young, blond-headed second boatman and guide for the day, dropped his fork, choking. He was having difficulty maintaining his nonchalance in the presence of celebrity.

Jud smiled and dug into his hotcakes.

The Laughing Trout

Suzanne continued: "I've written ninety seconds. We do an establishing shot between the two boats drifting in Box Canyon on the Snake River. When we're through we pick up twenty seconds of interview with the fish expert, Bosham. He meets us at Last Chance. We pick up thirty seconds of shots at different angles of the trout itself. We transmit to New York via an uplink to our local affiliate in Idaho Falls at 2:00 p.m.," she said.

Lulu and Pellegrini were relieved, thinking they might catch some sleep before reassignment or return to New York. A simple shoot, all arranged.

"However," continued Suzanne, "I saved the best for last."

Pellegrini and Dexter groaned.

"I talked with Goff this morning. New York wants *seven minutes for Sunday's 60/60*," she said excitedly, bouncing in her chair.

Pellegrini and Dexter groaned very loudly now.

Then Lulu Dexter smiled.

"Well, I'm really glad for ya, Suzanne," said Lulu.

"It's a big break," said Pellegrini. "Congrats, Suzanne. Remember your friends when you're the new anchor." He shook her hand.

"Just give me all you've got left in your overworked and underappreciated little souls, please?" said Suzanne to her crew. "This is important to me. Maybe we can even get the whole seven minutes wrapped by the end of the day," Suzanne said.

"Not likely," said Jud Buckalew, interrupting. "Look at that sky." Tendrils of gray cloud scudded in layers across the morning sun, breaking the light intermittently. "It's gonna rain."

"You said it rains almost every day," said Suzanne.

"It does. We often get afternoon thundershowers for an hour or so. But this looks like a front," said Buckalew.

Jud's Story

"Well then, let's get moving," said Suzanne.

Jud's boat drifted smoothly in the deep current of Box Canyon, the gray basalt cliffs sliding by quietly.

Suzanne Hsu stood in the bow of Jud's boat, her silver Patagonia jacket strategically unzipped to reveal just the proper amount of skin plunging into a pale blue flannel shirt. A lavaliere mike was clipped below the collar.

In the other boat, drifting a dozen feet to port, Don Pellegrini focused the video camera as Lulu Dexter monitored the dials of her audio system, sound muffs clapped over her head. The sun broke through the gathering clouds.

Pellegrini said, "Speed." Dexter dropped her hand. Hsu began:

"Here in Idaho's Snake River country, a strange tale of an odd fish continues to unfold—THREE, TWO, ONE—okay, we'll cut in the fish footage and Bosham interview here, keep the camera and sound running—THREE, TWO, ONE—Since Bosham was first to identify the fish, he is naming it after himself—*Onchorhynchis bosham* or Bosham's trout.

"The experts do not know what impact the new species may have on this famous stretch of fly-fishing river but they are deeply concerned, since the trout appears to be very aggressive.

"This is isolated country, not far from Yellowstone National Park. Yet every day, more and more fisherman come to try to catch one of these strange trout, for which a fifty thousand dollar reward has been offered.

"There's a hitch: it must be caught and kept alive.

"Bosham and other fish experts are hoping for some answers to their questions once they have a live specimen. Suzanne Hsu, NBC News in Island Park, Idaho." Pellegrini and Dexter looked at each other and nodded.

"It's a keeper," said Pellegrini across the water.

The Laughing Trout

Suzanne looked up at the sun as it wove through the streaming clouds.

"Let's do the promo for *60/60*," she said. "Jud, hold the mirror for me." Suzanne fluffed the hair back over her ears. Jud held the mirror while backing water with one oar.

"Okay. THREE, TWO, ONE," said Suzanne, standing again, arranging her jacket and mike.

"Speed," said Pellegrini.

Suzanne began: "A trout with fangs? A trout that may use its fins for walking? A trout that may stun its prey with sound? If it sounds fishy to you, watch *60/60* Sunday and find out why fish experts are scratching their heads and fishermen are racing for a fifty thousand dollar reward. That's Sunday on NBC's *60/60*."

Jud felt the first big droplet of rain splatter on his nose. In seconds, the rain was plunking into the boats and onto their shoulders. In Peter Pugmire's boat, Pellegrini and Dexter were covering their equipment. "Do you think this will last?" asked Suzanne anxiously.

"For a little while, probably," said Jud. He handed her a poncho from the boat locker. The rain now hissed into the Snake River, shattering its surface into dancing mirrorlets.

"Shit. There goes my hair," Suzanne cursed, pulling on the poncho.

A tremendous flash of light filled the Box Canyon, followed by an explosive crack of thunder that left the occupants of the two boats stunned and fearful.

The camera boat was now downstream two hundred yards from Jud's boat.

"PUT IN! PUT IN!" shouted Jud through the rain.

He began pulling vigorously on the oars, making for the south wall of the canyon. Suzanne was hunched in the bow, rain trickling off her nose and eyelashes. In the other boat,

Jud's Story

Peter was pulling toward the opposite shore. Jud's eyes raced down the shoreline for a place to land. The gray rock was impenetrable, solid. He pulled on the oars.

"Are we in danger?" called Suzanne.

"We're in a metal-trimmed boat on an open river in an electrical storm!" he shouted.

They rounded a cliff face. Jud could see a narrow sandbar between the rocks. But was there shelter? His eyes searched the cliff. In the rain, he saw a pine-clad ledge a hundred feet above the river. A dim game trail seemed to work through the rocks from the beach to the ledge. Jud stroked into the sandy spit and jumped from the boat as it grounded. He pulled the boat forward onto the sand with a mighty heave and tossed the anchor over for good measure.

Through the pelting rain, Jud could see the other boat far downstream. Peter was making for a cove.

Lightning and thunder spat into the canyon maliciously; a spiderweb of light caught the pine ridges for an instant. Then they were again lost in the rain and roar.

"Up here!" he shouted, helping Suzanne from the boat.

They splashed through the shallows. Jud picked his way up the cliff, almost dragging Suzanne behind him. They scrambled up the rocks, scraping knuckles and shins.

Jud helped Suzanne over the edge of the ledge and they darted under the spreading shelter of pine boughs. They were breathing hard. The pines had found a grip for their roots on the ledge. They had grown large over two centuries, laying down soft duff year after year. Beneath the protective boughs it was bone dry. Behind them, the cliff face blocked the wind.

Jud caught his breath and broke into a soft chuckle.

"Almost as nice as your own living room," he said.

"Talk about a port in a storm—" she said, looking at her surroundings as she shook out her hair.

The Laughing Trout

"Are you okay? I was kind of rough pulling you up here. We don't screw around with electrical storms," he said.

"My shins are barked, and my nose is running. The good news is that I didn't break a single fingernail," she said, laughing with relief at the relative comfort of the piney retreat.

They were silent for a few minutes as the wind returned to them. The rain continued, unabated.

"My feet got soaked. I'm getting cold," said Suzanne, rubbing her hands together.

Jud gathered a mound of pine needles and a few small, dry branches. From the tabbed pocket of the poncho he drew a bottle of safety matches. He struck a match to the little pile. In a moment, the needles sputtered and flared.

"The fire has the psychological effect of making me feel better, but I can't stop shaking," said Suzanne, shivering.

"C'mere," he said. He pulled the poncho over the woman's head, her greenish eyes looking up at him curiously.

He lifted his poncho and pulled her close to him, snuggling her to his side. Then he draped her poncho over both of them.

"We'll share our heat," he said. Jud could feel her heartbeat as he held her. Suzanne moved her arm across his chest and clung to him, shivering lightly.

"Pull your feet up," said Jud. He pulled off her wet shoes and stockings and began rubbing her feet with his free hand.

A furious burst of rain shook their tree. Suzanne pulled closer. Her hand moved up to his neck and rested softly below his ear.

For Jud it was like the moment between dream and awakening. It was ethereal, in slow-motion. A beautiful and famous woman was holding him tightly. She was cold and a little frightened.

Jud's Story

Jud had an uncontrollable urge to kiss her. Panic rose and fell within him as he thought of what would happen if he did. What if she shouted NO! Or what if she simply looked up with alarm and said: "That's very unprofessional, Mr. Buckalew."

But what if she really *wanted* to be kissed? What if he missed that centimeter of chance the gods offer once in a lifetime? Suzanne Hsu resolved the question: "Is there something wrong with me?" she queried, lifting her mouth to him.

"Oh, no," said Jud hastily, fumbling for composure beneath the ponchos.

"Then kiss me," she said directly, moving both her hands up to hold his face.

Jud kissed her tentatively; she responded by opening her mouth. They kissed deeply. Her hands went under his shirt and began softly caressing his chest, touching his nipples.

"I'm supposed to be doing that," he murmured."Then do it," she demanded, thrusting her breasts into his hands.

"Mmmmmmmm, Jud," she said. "You are delicious."

"And you are very beautiful and very, very sexy and, God, I may never survive this," said Jud.

"You better survive," she panted. "Because I may want more of this." She looked directly into his eyes, her tongue moving over her teeth and lips.

The wind howled. Fountains and fires and great spasms surged as they melted together. Jud pulled her tightly against him as Suzanne gripped him in her dancer's legs. They shook with pleasure. The rain shook off the sheltering pines. More, and more, and more.

"It's a long time since I last made love," murmured Jud.

"You don't seem to have forgotten anything," said Suzanne, smiling up into his eyes.

The Laughing Trout

It was ninety minutes before they rejoined the others. Lulu cocked her head curiously as they climbed from the boat. Jud and Suzanne passed a knowing look between them—aware that at least Lulu knew what had happened between them. But neither cared.

"Just stand there and let me look at you," said Jud. Suzanne was naked, coming out of his bathroom.

She stood silhouetted in the light, a dancer's tight buttocks and small, firm breasts perched high. He could see the bikini line high on her thigh. She switched off the light and with her dancer's walk moved softly to Jud on the bed. Outside the clouds were scudding past the moon. Jud heard nighthawks screeching over the sound of the river.

"You couldn't tell I wanted you?" she said. "Even last night I wanted you."

"Maybe you want to screw all the men you meet on your assignments. Being hit on is common for guides up here," said Jud.

"I could be really pissed off at that," said Suzanne.

"Look. I've gotta be straight with you," said Jud, raising up on his elbows from the shadows of the pillow.

"Suzanne, you are a shock to my simple, isolated life. You are famous. You are beautiful. You've chosen *me*, Jud Buckalew, and I find that hard to believe."

"So do I, Jud," Suzanne said, brushing her hair back over her gold earloops as she looked down on Jud's lean body.

"You're saying this isn't just a little extra-curricular diversion from work?" said Jud, looking at her eyes for a sign.

"I had these very strong feelings for you the first time I saw you, at Vera's dancing."

Jud's Story

"And you can just understand your feelings like that? Hell, I've spent forty years trying to understand my feelings," he said, shaking his head with disbelief.

"I know myself. I owe that to my Scotch-Irish mother and her hard-edged approach to reality. How well do you know yourself?" she said.

"Better now than ever before. Gained at the expense of considerable pain," said Jud, flopping back on the pillow. Suzanne snuggled in next to him, her breasts against his side.

"If I'm going to fall in love with you, I must know all about you," she said, kissing him softly on the lips. Jud looked at her, unspeaking, for a long time.

Bob the cat bounded to the bed and began kneading a place for himself in the rumpled covers.

"Everything about me?" he said.

First he told her about growing up in Paris. The words came slowly, prompted from time to time by her questions.

Yes, his father—editor of the Montpelier *Tribune*—died when Jud was eleven. It was a big shock. There was no money, except to bury his father. His mother had gone to work for Mark Bosham's father, thankful for a job that enabled her and her son to stay in Paris, yet ever-fearful of what the future might again hand her. She had put high hopes in Jud for her old age security. She became so intent on Jud's becoming successful that she lost the ability to express the love she felt for her son.

Jud knew it was there but hidden in the folds of her fear, virtually lost during Jud's descent into alcohol.

Only in the last year had her cards and letters been signed "Love, Mother."

He loved her, but for now he did not like her much.

The Laughing Trout

Jud realized she was recovering, just as he was, and that it might be some time before there was a comfortable equilibrium.

"There was trouble—something to do with Mark, right?" said Suzanne.

"Yes. Mark was held up to me as a paragon of faith, virtue, and intellect. Yet in fact he was sort of a Henry Kissinger, cunning, devious, and a suck-ass sycophant.

"From our early days, we had been competitive. We had a yearly fishing contest that never ended, really. I would try to escape to fish on my own, and he would try to find out where I went to catch fish. I usually was way ahead of him in the contest, although I suspect he was keeping up by devious means—like once I caught him exploding an M-80 firecracker in one of the most productive fishing holes on Swan Creek. All the trout were stunned, floating belly-up on the surface where Mark could pick 'em up.

"When I was ten, I built a secret tree hut that hung in a cottonwood over St. Charles Creek. I camouflaged it and kept its location all to myself. Over the next few years, I watched the trout living and feeding in the river below my hut. I got to know them individually. Each trout is as individual as a snowflake, you know. I watched them feed, sleep, fight, and fornicate. I knew where Isabel would be feeding at sunset and where Ike would be sleeping at noon. I spent hours watching, listening to the creek—and mourning my father. I fell in love with `troutness' over those years.

"One spring morning a great, dark shadow drifted slowly into the pool. I called it The Battleship, it was so big. The Battleship was a female cutthroat trout, come upstream from Bear Lake to spawn. I watched her scarlet throat flashes as she scooped out her redd—her nest—in the pebbles of the stream bottom. She lay there depositing her eggs, softly

Jud's Story

fanning against the current as the eggs poured into nest. She had a lovely, big ivory eye. She was all gold and steel, with distinct black spots down her back. She always brought a smaller male with her. They sort of wrapped around each other like they were in love, then he would move over the redd and deposit his sperm in spasmodic orgasms.

"Four springs I watched this. By then Mark had decided he wanted to share the only real talent I was noted for in town—the knowledge of trout. It was my very essence. The one thing that really defined me.

Trout were something I threw myself into. A fantasy escape from the reality of my dad's death.

"Mark started sucking up to me when he saw that his old man admired my knowledge. He did that any time his old man found anything praiseworthy of me. He couldn't stand to see me getting praise. You know, Mark's smart. It's just that he's amoral—" Jud stopped, his thoughts deep in memories of his past.

"Go on," said Suzanne, enchanted by fish poetry.

"Mark came on being very nice to me. Almost as nice as when he wanted to use my .22 to shoot cats, but that's another story. He convinced me to show him my hut. Like a fool, I did. And like a fool, I invited him to come the day I expected the Battleship to spawn. We waited, watching. Sure enough, up she came and began her ritual. Mark jumped when he saw her size."Now I had sworn Mark to secrecy, but that very afternoon, the little bastard took a net into the hole and dipped out that big, beautiful trout.

"I found out about it when I went into Mike's—that's the local bar and cafe—where the guys were gathered round lookin' at the big fish's carcass," said Jud. He stroked Suzanne's hair as he would pet Bob.

"So what did you do?" said Suzanne.

The Laughing Trout

"The trouble was I didn't do anything. I was furious and angry but I didn't dare say or do anything.

I was afraid of angering my mother and my uncle—and of not being accepted in the community. I just stuffed those feelings and let 'em simmer."

"So that's what caused all the animosity?" she asked.

"The beginning of it. When Mark heard I was going to Utah State to study fisheries management, he promptly announced that was his goal, too. And my mother was insistent that I give Mark all the help I could. She was felt obligated to Mark's father, her employer.

"So I shared. I showed him all my data on brown trout. I had this youthful and probably correct theory that brown trout were harder to catch because before they were imported to America they had been under fishing pressure in Europe for a thousand years," Judd said.

"And brown trout had a genetic memory?" she said, snuggling closely.

"Yeah, basically," he said, smiling with surprise as he looked at her. "I monitored tagged cutthroat trout and browns for three summers. You could catch the cutthroat six times each summer. The brown, only two times."

"Now I've got to jump from trout to a woman," he sighed.

"By the time I was a senior I had fallen in love.

Her name was Beth Pierce, a beautiful redhead from Preston and homecoming queen in her junior year. Well, we got married, I was graduated with honors. I wanted to go to graduate school, but it would have been costly.

"I was weighing graduate school when the Idaho Fish and Game Department offered me a good job in Stanley, so I took it. Beth and I were very happy for those first couple of years.

Jud's Story

We lived in this funny little trailer away from everything. Once a week we'd go into Ketchum and splurge...

"Well, I had experienced the joys of beer during my freshman year. I'd never tasted alcohol until college.

Wow. It was like the stuff made everything right. I was fear-free, outgoing, and exceptionally clever after a few beers.

"I was going on these little bats, little benders that started on Fridays and ended Sunday night. Beth was unhappy about it. I figured that maybe a location change would cure my fixation for weekend alcohol. So I put in for a transfer to Bear Lake. And I got it. Bear Lake was potentially a very fine fishery. But it wasn't ever able to support survivable pools of planted fish, and for various reasons the natural reproduction rate for cutthroat trout was quite low. We always knew it could support a lot of fish if we could get them to survive as fingerlings," Jud continued.

"Is this boring you?" he said, lifting himself on one elbow and looking down at the soft, tan body with intrigued eyes.

"No. You could never bore me. Go on," said Suzanne.

"Well, I got assigned to Bear Lake. So did Mark—as my boss—having just emerged with his master's degree "I was stunned to learn that he had used my brown trout data for his thesis. He promised that when the time was right I would be properly acknowledged, etcetera, etcetera. But there were my data and my theory presented as his own."

"Didn't your old professors recognize this?"

"They knew I'd been working on the question, but assumed that, since I'd gotten married and left college, I'd lost interest in further pursuit of an advanced degree. And Mark was my cousin. Everyone knew that in the department. It's a small school. They just assumed everything Mark did was okay with me. And by then my boozing was making me feel just guilty enough to not make waves. It was kind of an alcohol psychosis that robbed me of my integrity and motivation. It was easier to hope Mark would keep his word.

"Anyway, we moved back to Paris; and for the next few years, I worked on the Bear Lake stocking question, with Mark always looking over my shoulder. I played into his hands even more. Once, when we went to a fisheries department meeting, I got drunk and didn't show up for an important section. Mark never let me forget that. He said he couldn't trust me. Hell, I couldn't trust myself. So of course I kept giving him access to all my research.

"Year after year, in addition to my other duties, I studied the lake. I would go out twice a day in a boat and take temperature soundings. I learned there were thermal layers in Bear Lake. If fingerling cutthroat were planted when the top layer was a dead-even fifty degrees, and when the secondary layer was about thirty feet below, the fingerlings survived. It was because the combination of water layering kept the predator Mackinaw trout and Bonneville cisco feeding below the second, colder layer. This allowed the young fingerlings adequate time to disperse and find natural cover. The survival ratio went up significantly. The key was the timing of the temperature."

"All this Mark stole?"

"Yes. But not until he thought I was out of the way."

"Out of the way?" asked Suzanne.

"Ummm. I was still drinking. Beth was now unhappily aware that she had married an alcoholic. As the years passed, she pulled away from me, although she said she still loved me. She refused to have kids, however. We quarreled more frequently." Jud was quiet.

"Go on," urged Suzanne.

"I don't know if I want to," said Jud. He was quiet for a long time. The rain started pattering on the cabin roof. Bob

Jud's Story

purred with a bumblebee-hum. Suzanne nestled her cheek on his chest.

"It was a cool but sunny spring day five years ago. Beth had scrimped and saved enough so that we could buy a house of our own, and we'd made a contract with the owner of the place. Now it was moving day. I went down to Mike's Cafe to find some folks to help me move. That's the way you do it in little Idaho towns. Folks pitch in and help. It was a Saturday and lots of the farm and ranch help were gathered already drinking beer. I said I needed some help and got plenty of volunteers with pickups. Have a beer first, they said, so I said okay.

"Six hours later we got to my place. I could hardly stand up, yet I carried a twelve-pack into the old house, drinking as I tried to help Beth finish packing."Then I passed out. What did the good ol' boys do?

They set my passed-out body up in a chair in the back of a pickup and drove me off to the new house. But before they got there, of course they had to stop for a few more at Mike's. Mike's is in the middle of town. I'm passed out in a chair in the back of the truck and the whole county is driving by 'cause Saturday is the day they come to town to market."

"It sounds humiliating," said Suzanne.

"That was *good* part of the day," said Jud softly.

He looked away from Suzanne, up at the ceiling.

"I came to after sunset, still sitting in the back of the truck at Mike's, sunburned and raw. Drunk as I still was, it occurred to me that I'd better get over to the new house to see how Beth was going to take this. I bought another six-pack and drove the truck to the house. When I got there, Beth was away some where. There were boxes stacked up.

"I remember sitting on the kitchen floor with the six pack. I remember thinking that the money for the down payment

The Laughing Trout

was in an envelope in the glove box of the truck. My mind started to work on that money. You see," he said softly, still looking at the ceiling, "we had saved ninety four hundred dollars over the years just for this. It was all in cash, ninety four one hundred dollar bills in an envelope, because Mr. Garn, the man from whom we were buying the place, was a cattle dealer and after we closed with him Sunday morning he was going to Cache Valley to a cattle auction. He insisted on cash because the banks would be closed.

"So I sat there on the kitchen floor, worrying about what Beth was going to say about my getting so drunk on moving day, and I became paranoid about that money. I remember going to the truck to make sure it wasn't stolen while I was passed out. The money was still there. So then I decided it wasn't safe in the truck. So I hid it."

"Where?" said Suzanne quietly.

"Damned if I know," said Jud with a catch in his voice.

"I dug up the yard, tore apart everything. I spent a month trying to find that cash. It never turned up." Beth simply walked out that Sunday morning. She has refused to see me ever since. I can't blame her," Jud said slowly.

"She wouldn't forgive you?"

"It was too late for that. You see, there was another incident about money that happened before. I stayed out all night and came home with $760 in my pocket.

"To this day I don't know where that came from. That's just as terrifying, for me. What did I do to get that money?" Jud sighed.

"In a few days, I realized Beth was gone for good and that I was the disgrace of the town. I drifted here to try to sober up. Island Park always soothed me as a kid. And Mark figured I was out of the picture for good," Jud added.

"That's ancient history, Jud," said Suzanne. "We're here now, together. You can never reclaim the past. Let go of all of it. I love you. I love you truly and passionately."

Jud looked into Suzanne's eyes. He felt an honesty as certain as sunrise. For the first time in years, Jud felt light and happy, like a freed balloon.

CHAPTER TWENTY-TWO

Never Assume

In Cheyenne, Colonel Herbert Hoover Sponzini meticulously punched figures into the large calculator sitting next to his breakfast plate.

He had sliced his four sausages into sixteen perfectly equal portions. His two pieces of rye toast were quartered. The scrambled eggs were neatly portioned into eighths. One bite of sausage, followed by a one eighth of egg mounded on a pallet of toast, followed again by one bite of sausage. Carefully chewed and swallowed, the cycle started again. Sausage, egg and toast. It was a comforting and familiar morning rhythm.

"More coffee?" said the waitress, yawning at the blue-gray light of dawn creeping above the flatlands of eastern Wyoming.

"No thank you. I'll get the jitters," said Sponzini in a warning tone. The waitress shrugged indifferently at the narrow-faced man whose slipping black hair formed a crescent

The Laughing Trout

around the sides of his shiny, tan head. She moved on to the next table at the Lamplighter Best Western Restaurant.

Sponzini was pleasantly surprised at his mileage on the last leg of this trip. Two hundred twenty two miles from North Platte, Nebraska. Eleven point two six nine miles to the gallon—the best he had done since the leg between Oklahoma City and Dodge City. The calculator said he would need nineteen point seven gallons to top his truck tank.

What was bothering him right now was the unanswered question: Would the southern route—through New Mexico, Arizona, then up through Nevada and Utah—have saved time and money? He'd calculated several times that the central route through Texas, Oklahoma, Nebraska, and Wyoming would be somewhat faster and shorter. But he'd learned years ago never to trust Rand McNally when it came to real accuracy. They were not military maps. The Colonel prided himself on his map reading. And there was this big question. Should he return via the southerly route? It could prove much longer and more costly, but then he would know the answer about the distance; of course, this would make him regret not having gone with his original strategy.

If he returned on the route he now traveling, Herbert Hoover Sponzini might never know the answer, and that bothered him, too. Why, there could be a difference of a hundred—perhaps a hundred and fifty—miles.

"A careful engineer never assumes," he could hear his father's voice, the product of years of directing the work of open-pit coal mining. "Because 'assume', if you look at the word, makes an ass of 'u' and 'me'."

He crunched down on the egg-toast segment of his breakfast cycle and tried to forget the troubling route quandary.

Back to the map. At sixty miles an hour, his truck, with its seventeen-foot boat and trailer, would make Salt Lake

City in about seven hours and twenty minutes, if he did not stop. Sponzini wrote these figures down in a leather-bound notebook; he would want to compare them with the actual elapsed time upon arrival.

Oh-oh, he thought, glancing from note pad to map. It looks as if I'll have to cross—what are they called—the Snowy Range? He tapped the line marking the mountains. And then the Wasatch Mountains. Maybe I'd better factor that at eight hours even. He thought scribbled in his notepad, then returned to his breakfast, savoring the rubbery chewiness of the sausage.

Sponzini looked again at the newspaper clipping neatly folded inside the cover of the notepad. "Fifty thousand dollars," he whispered to himself between munches. "Well, let a real bass man show them a thing or two about catching trout," he muttered aloud. Trout fishermen did not have live wells in their boats.

"What about bass and trout?" said the waitress, pausing as she heard him muttering.

She plopped the back of her hand on her hip and laughed at Sponzini. "Talking to yourself mister? Think nothin' of it. I do it all the time," she said with a smile and a wave.

Sponzini flushed crimson with chagrin.

He hurriedly ate the remainder of his breakfast and double-checked the figures on his restaurant bill with his calculator. He paid the tab and went into the restaurant bathroom where he pulled a dental kit from his pocket and brushed his teeth. Now properly prepared, he strode toward his rig, anxious to check out the truck and boat before the day's drive got underway.

CHAPTER TWENTY THREE

Ownership's Heavy Responsibilities

Frieda and Cuss Cox had spent three inauspicious—perhaps portentous—days struggling with the new pickup and boat.

Somehow the electrical system in the new pickup was malfunctioning. As Frieda jiggled happily along Interstate 15 near the Idaho border, Cuss noticed the negative reading on the electrical gauge. He returned to the nearest large town, Brigham City, where the Dodge dealer solicitously took his truck into the service bay. A mechanic tinkered under the hood all afternoon, replaced a computer chip, and handed the keys back to Cox.

They spent the night at the Crystal Springs KOA and departed before dawn, again heading north on the Interstate.

"Shitshitshit!" said Cox as the gauge again died, and the motor began to miss. He pulled into the Dodge dealer's bay

The Laughing Trout

in Idaho Falls, where they told him a part would have to be ordered from Salt Lake.

They limped to a campground and spent Sunday fishing from the bank of the Snake River just north of town, Frieda sitting beneath a broad-rimmed straw hat in a folding chair, her plump knuckles tightly gripping her favorite spinning rod.

The next morning, it was a wealthier auto dealer who bid the Coxes goodbye as they continued toward Island Park.

At noon, Frieda shouted: "There's a good place!"

Cuss pulled the truck onto soft grass in a low area on an inlet of Island Park Reservoir. The lake winked prismic reflections as the gentle midday wind coursed its surface.

During the stop-and-go journey to Island Park, they had had plenty of time to discuss the strategy for catching Bosham's trout.

"That fish has got to live in the reservoir," said Cuss. Frieda agreed. They were reservoir fishers. If anyone could catch fish in reservoirs, the Coxes could.

"Let's get 'em," said Frieda, a bucket for their catch in her hand. Cuss maneuvered the trailer onto the boat ramp. In a moment, the aluminum boat tugged gently at its mooring line as Frieda and Cuss piled it high with gear.

"My, that's beautiful," said Frieda as she watched the boat roll gently on the incoming waves. "We ought to give her a name, Rulon," she said thoughtfully.

How about Rulon's Bellyache, she thought, smiling inside, but not daring to suggest it aloud.

Cuss gave the motor mount a final twist, biting it into the unblemished transom.

"That ought to hold it," he said. "C'mon." He steadied the boat as Frieda clambered in, dropping the freeboard by several inches.

Ownership's Heavy Responsibilities

By now wary of things mechanical, Cuss prayed the new motor would be trouble-free. He primed it, moved the lever to START and pulled the rope.

BRRRRRRRRRRrrrrrrrrrr. The motor roared to life. Frieda clapped her hands, nearly losing her big, floppy hat when she let go of it.

Slowly Cuss reversed from the landing, avoiding the dozen small boats tied to moorages. He moved the lever to FORWARD and they shot off across Island Park Reservoir toward the inlet. In a few minutes, they were letting out line behind the slow-moving boat as it chugged at trolling speed into the chop. Cuss turned on the electronic fish-finder, which glowed green. He located a dozen fish around the thirty-foot level. They watched the colored sections of the line drop into the dark water at intervals. Cuss fished at forty feet; Frieda at twenty feet. Silently, Team Reservoir bracketed the unwary Bosham's trout school, raising and lowering the depth of their lures, passing through the thermocline.

By 4:00 p.m., they had caught and released a dozen common rainbow trout.

"Let's go over by the dam," said Frieda. Cuss gunned the outboard and the boat lifted its bow and bounced across the waves, leaving an arrow-straight wake of which Cuss was visibly proud.

"Yer doin' so good, Cuss!" said Frieda, holding her dress down with one hand, her hat on with the other.

They trolled for an hour. Frieda intently studied her rod. Suddenly it arced downward with a thud she could feel clear to her shoulders. She struck. She connected with a solid object.

"I got a big one," she said excitedly. She reeled in ten feet of line. The fish ripped it back out and dived. A moment

The Laughing Trout

later, the line went limp as the fish raced for the surface and broke water in a high leap.

The big rainbow hung an instant in the evening light, water spinning from its shaking body.

"Wa-hooo!" shouted Frieda.

"Damnhell!" said Cuss.

Ten minutes later Frieda clipped the rainbow to the stringer and trailed it over the side of the boat. Flushed and shaking with excitement, Frieda wiped her hands. Cuss looked thoughtful.

"Now that's a mighty nice fish," said Cuss. "But it ain't the fish we're after. Whaddya say we pull the boat up on the dam, go down to the spillway, and fish where the water pours out. Just until dusk. We can start trolling again early tomorrow."

The fly fisherman might not have tried the turbulent torrent at the dam outlet, Cuss reasoned.

They pulled the boat up so it couldn't drift off.

With light spinning equipment and folding chairs, they picked their way down a trail to the spillway, Cuss letting Frieda carry the heavy tackle boxes.

They settled at the tail of the racing water where it roared on its rush to the Pacific. The couple fished silently. They could not hear each other's voices over the rush of the water.

They caught nothing. As the sun dipped below the pines Cuss signaled Frieda to reel in. They collected their gear and slowly made their way back up the trail.

"Shitpissasshole!" roared Cuss as they came to the boat. The outboard motor was missing.

"It's gone!" said Frieda.

"Goddamn right it's gone. Some bastards stole our brand-new motor!" yelled aid Cuss, looking across the lake, suspiciously eyeing the boats working its surface in the evening light.

Ownership's Heavy Responsibilities

Cuss rowed across the lake toward the harbor, skipping epithets like flat rocks over the wave tops.

Frieda cried a little as she thought of the shiny, new motor. Oh well, they could afford another.

CHAPTER TWENTY-FOUR

Just Another Morning in the Woods

Christopher Gurney Cochran, ex-convict and angry eco-freak, awakened at the crack o' noon.

He was hot. His head lay next to the tire of his car. The sun beat down on his sleeping bag, reflecting off the yellow Volkswagen, despite its heavy impasto of dust and grime from endless western trails. Lodgepole pines bowed over on him, as if in sympathy about his sweaty brow and queasy stomach.

After his release from the Livingston Jail, he had driven to Island Park, stopping several times for celebratory beers at the little wayside taverns along Route 20 as it wound through Montana and south into Idaho. It had been very late when he pulled into the campground, and he had promptly stretched out alongside his car.

The Laughing Trout

Cochran was aware of loud thumping sounds coming from not too far away. He could hear a river. And it seemed to be shouting *Don't want to go to rehab, no, no, no....*

He squinted at the sun. It burned into his skull and set off rockets over each ear. His tongue felt huge and hairy. The three-day stubble on his chin rasped on the fabric of the sleeping bag. Without getting from his bag, Cochran pulled himself to the car and opened its door.

He fumbled for his shaving kit, found two aspirin, and gulped them down with water from a plastic jug.

He dragged himself to the shade of a low pine. In a minute, he was feeling better. The gas in his gut was subsiding, too. He felt as if he could fart "Hail to the Chief." Oh well, a man didn't get out of jail every day.

Walk like an Egyptian, sang the river. Cochran blinked. He shook his head lightly. Damn ears, he thought, wiggling a finger in each one. Playing tricks on me.

Down on me! the river belted out this song. It was like a needle in Cochran's mind. It was *not* his imagination. Music was blaring out, echoing through the gentle pines, drowning out the whiffle of the river, shitting in his already-befouled morning psyche. Cochran climbed from the sleeping bag. He stealthily moved toward his car and groped for the sledge hammer he kept under the hood. Lovingly he cradled this gift from his grandfather, a World War II tank driver who had taught the boy both rabid conservation concepts and fearlessness. Holding the sledge hammer behind him, he peered in the direction of the sound. It seemed to come from the river. He moved through the pines, darting for cover behind each tree. Then Cochran saw the source: the open doors of a Toyota pickup truck, alongside which sat two young men in web chairs eating sandwiches as they took their lunch break.

Just Another Morning in the Woods

They bounced their feet in time to the music and munched ham and cheese.

"JEEEEEEZZ, WHAT'S THIS?!" shouted the shorter, fatter of the young fisherman as he toppled backward in his chair, dexterously saving the potato chip in his grip.

The leaner man turned just in time to see the specter emerge from the forest—a long-haired youth with crazed bloodshot eyes, wearing grimy, rumpled clothes, lurching toward them and waving a sledge hammer.

"Stand back!" said Cochran sonorously as he strode up to the truck, oblivious to the wide-eyed fishermen who were trying to get out of his way. He imagined himself a Northwest Mounted Policeman trying to save the innocent pines from the Attack of the Great Angst.

BLAM! The head of the sledge drove into the dashboard. Dust flew from inside the open truck. Shards of plastic and metal flew across the cab. Wires erupted from the dashboard. Smoke rose in a gentle curl from the music player. Then there was silence.

"There. That'll take care of it," said Cochran as he saluted the fishermen with a wave of the sledge hammer, then turned to walk back through the woods to his VW. The sound of the dashboard shattering made him uneasy, not for having behaved inappropriately, but because it further polluted the aural beauty of the forest and river.

He was aware of the distant shouts of the fishermen as he climbed into the Volkswagen and fired it up. A raven flew down from his post in a dead spruce and stroked parallel with Christopher as he shifted into gear on the pavement of Route 20.

"Cochran," he thought heard the raven say, "heroism feels and never reasons and therefore is always right."

CHAPTER TWENTY-FIVE

Cochran's Ploy

Dodick and Okleberry were two of twenty-two fishermen who formed a long, loose line below Coffee Pot Rapid. The fishermen silently stroked their lines forward in false casts, then shot them with various proficiencies out over the flow to settle in eddies and runs of the Snake. Occasionally there would be a splash, and a line would tighten.

"Did she sound pissed?" shouted the moon-faced farmer over the sound of the rushing water. He couldn't take his mind off Dodick's call to Okleberry's wife, Judy, to tell her they were staying an extra day. Okleberry didn't dare do it himself; he was too drunk, and she'd know it, although he thought about blaming it on cell phone reception.

"She wanted to know just how drunk you were," Dodick shouted back.

"Oh, God," Okleberry gulped. There were no secrets from his wife.

The Laughing Trout

After a dozen beers at lunch, they had felt it might be prudent if each called the other's wife. The story each gave was that the fishing was so good that the partner was this very minute out landing lunkers. Why, they expected to catch the Bosham trout this very afternoon.

Dodick's wife, Bev, had simply hung up on Okleberry.

But Okleberry's wife, Judy, wanted to savor her husband's discomfort and fear of her sharp tongue. She whipsawed Dodick verbally for a couple uncomfortable minutes."Thanks," said a grateful Okleberry, spared the ignominy.

"You want another beer?" shouted Dodick."Yeah," said Okleberry.

Dodick pulled two beers from the fish-keeper in his vest, tossing one to his partner. At that instant, a twelve-inch rainbow chomped on his drifting number fourteen pale morning dun fly and spat the hook before Dodick could pull the belly from his line. He giggled.

"Just missed Bosham's trout," he yelled, tipping the sudsy can to his lips.

His eye caught something in its peripheral vision. He turned to look behind him. A naked man stood on the bank. He had no way of knowing it was Christopher Cochran, ex-con, nature-lover, and eco-terrorist. What Dodick did know was that an unshaven, wild-eyed young man was perched atop a large rock, singing "It's a Small World" at the top of his lungs as he fondled his penis.

The fishermen—one-by-one—turned to view the spectacle. Cochran launched into "R-E-S-P-E-C-T," shaking his white buttocks at the stunned fishermen.

Disgusted fishermen began wading ashore. A worried woman in a camper pulled her children inside and closed the door hurriedly. Explorers and Yukons and Outbacks sped away from the campground. The doors to trailers—Bounders, Rascals, and Prowlers—thumped shut as their shocked owners hooked them up for a haul to anywhere else.

Now Cochran lifted a bottle of cooking oil and rubbed it all over his body as he belted out a chorus of "Beware of the Naked Man."

Cochran, fully oiled, leaped into the river from his rock and began swimming downstream, past the few remaining fishermen, directly through the finest trout run at Coffee Pot.

"Hi there! ... Hello! ... Good afternoon!" He greeted each disbelieving fisherman as he floated past. All but Dodick and Okleberry reeled in their lines and fled the river, threatening and cursing. Dodick and Okleberry stood in drunken disbelief, lines and jaws slack as they stared at the nude swimmer.

He stroked with the current to reach Dodick and Okleberry, splashing and kicking.

"Say," shouted Cochran, "I could scout the bottom for you."

"We were just leaving," said a wide-eyed Dodick. "Don't you think we need to go get some beer, Gordon?" he added with all the nonchalance he could muster.

"Yeah," gulped Okleberry.

The farmer and the implement salesman were the last to exit Coffee Pot Rapid, leaving it entirely to a crazed, naked man, who now had cleared the area totally of human beings.

The naked Cochran hummed happily as he climbed on a large, dark rock, feeling its warmth against his naked legs and bottom. He just knew the trout were this very minute thanking him.

CHAPTER TWENTY-SIX

Sparks

A million questions raced through the mind of Colonel Herbert Hoover Sponzini as the truck made the long pull from Ashton up the grade to Island Park. Logistics, materiel, these were just words to most people, but Sponzini had lived them during his military years. His had been a tidy, impeccable life, lived by the clock and by the book. It was a comfort to know exactly what he would be doing at sixteen hundred hours, or at zero seven hundred.

That was one of the problems of change: it required new rules, new checklists, much time and energy expended. Just now he was experiencing the agony of change as the reality of arrival at his destination loomed just minutes away. Questions, big questions: like what kind of a place would his quarters be. After a web search from the Super 8 Motel in Salt Lake City he had been able to book a room at a place with the vaguely suspicious name of The Laughing Trout.

The Laughing Trout

"It's my place or your tent," snorted a woman on the other end of the line who said she was Vera. She explained that, because of the "current trout frenzy," her place had the only room left in the area and she assured him the vacancy would not last long. He took it.

Sponzini shuddered at the thought of a tent. After Vietnam, he vowed never to set foot in a tent—or a war zone—again. The military is a career, not a misery. He had kept that vow as he came to realize that materiel and logistics officers do not live in tents, and are kept very busy far behind the action making sure things keep flowing to the valorous boys on the line. He had, after all, proved himself in combat, even if it was a fluke that a PFC had sent a rifle slug through his buttocks as if piercing twin melons. It was the ignominy that had hurt most.

The truck surged forward, freed of the grade as it cleared the hill below the Railroad Ranch. This was new country for Sponzini. Pines dotted open sagebrush plains where a big river looped back on itself. He could see fishermen standing like posts in the river, their stick arms thrust forward anxiously, flicking lines endlessly.

"Too much work," he thought. And even if he wanted to, that sleazy Houston doctor had warned him against wading. Maintain a checklist on your body, just like your vehicle—and your life will be prolonged, he thought with satisfaction.

But questions still bothered him as he slowed at Last Chance. What would he eat tonight? Could he get enough greens? What about onions? He had to watch onions. They brought on flatulence. And there were license requirements. And then he would have somehow learn the locally popular lures.

The Laughing Trout loomed into view. Not much to look at, he thought, but was consoled by the knowledge that it would not be very expensive. Or would it? There were a lot of people demanding rooms and demand, as every logistician knew, forced prices up.

Sponzini parked the truck, climbed from the cab, smoothed his shirt over his stomach and ran a comb through the shiny black bumpers of his hair. He looked at his teeth in the rear-view mirror, adjusted his belt, and headed through the door.

Vera Segura could only see Colonel Sponzini in silhouette as he stood in the doorway. Ramrod straight, thin-hipped, straight-shouldered.

"You've gotta be Colonel Sponzini," she said directly.

"I am. How did you know?" said the surprised man.

"'Cause cowboys and timber cruisers don't walk at attention," she said, looking him over slowly.

He flushed, unable to find an appropriate response.

"You have my room ready I presume?"

"Sure," she said, looking the man over as she would have examined a side of beef she was buying for the cafe.

The man vaguely reminded her of Owen, her second husband, a Marine flight mechanic from El Toro. Always liked that tight-ass military bearing, she thought. It was such fun to see it shattered once they had their clothes off. She remember how Owen would come through the door of the apartment at the end of each day, put his left hand around her neck and his right hand down her pants first thing. Then he would kiss her. Sometimes they never did get dinner in those early days, she sighed. Direct men, these military types. She shook off her thoughts. They were making her face warm.

She walked Sponzini to Cabin 4 and swung open the door, standing against it with her full breasts tilted up like cannons.

The Laughing Trout

Sponzini had to squeeze past Vera with his bags, his chest lightly brushing Vera's nipples as he passed.

Sponzini pretended he brushed breasts every day like this, whistling as he unzipped his bags.

"Everything's all right?" she said.

"This will be fine," he answered, his attention focused on his bags.

She stood watching Sponzini carefully unpack his clothing, hanging jackets, fishing clothes, and khaki trousers neatly in the pine closet. She noted that he placed work shoes, leather boots, athletic shoes, rubber boots in a tidy row.

"If there's anything you want, just give a whistle," she said. "*Anything.*"

He mumbled, not daring to look up.

As Vera left, she noticed that the Colonel was lining up his vitamin pills alphabetically on the dresser top. She giggled to herself. This guy interested her. All it would take is one little teeny tiny crack in his armor and *zow!* She knew the type.

CHAPTER TWENTY-SEVEN

The Day's Events

Toward sunset that day there was a traffic jam at Mack's Inn. An elderly woman from Ogden, Utah, became angry and shattered the window of a honking pickup truck by throwing a jar of her strawberry preserves against it. A family from Eugene, Oregon, reported a naked singer at Coffee Pot Rapid. The missus, an opera buff, said she was certain he was singing "The Entry March" from *Aida.*

Beal Finnegan's Last Chance Gas and Tackle ran out of non-resident fishing licenses. The store at Pond's Lodge ran out of bread and milk. Vera's ran out of Bud, Millers, and Schlitz. Wine coolers were getting low. A short fisherman from Reno stormed into the Idaho Fish and Game Office and angrily reported that a naked man had swum through his fishing radius at Coffee Pot Rapid, singing "Captain Jiggs of the Horse Marines."

Two frightened students from Boise reported the death of an in-dash stereo and CD player from causes due to sledge

The Laughing Trout

hammer blows. The assailant, they said, was courteous and helpful, if somewhat estranged from their tastes in music.

A wide-eyed young fisherman from New Haven reported accidentally hooking a naked man in the Snake River as the man struck at his fly. He lost a size sixteen Tango Triumphant to the seedy-looking swimmer who was singing "Never Gonna Let You Go."

A skinny little middle-aged Salt Lake City man, screeching vile oaths of retribution, reported an outboard motor stolen from his boat while it was beached at Island Park Reservoir.

Mark Harvey Bosham set up an electric shocking grid and hired six men to move slowly down the Snake, shocking fish to the surface so he could examine each one. He was excitedly determined to bring up his namesake trout by wholesale means.

Jud Buckalew told Suzanne Hsu of hunting feral cats to collect a dollar bounty offered by his Uncle Bernard Bosham. He made $80 one year. Bob was his first attempt to make amends to the feline race. Suzanne kissed Jud Buckalew, touched by his string of painful admissions.

CHAPTER TWENTY-EIGHT

Whoops

Col. Sponzini reigned magisterially over his big bassboat, twenty glittering feet of anodized aluminum whorls. It had been the project of his dreams, executed as precisely as meshing gears.

Directing a metal shop to construct him a comfortable pedestal chair that could be raised and lowered and tilted back for comfort, Sponzini then commissioned an auto upholstery specialist to design a leaping gold bass in the royal blue leather seat. A matching blue seatbelt was installed, and the chair was then bolted to the deck.

Foot pedals and an upright console at his right hand gave him speed and direction control over the stern-mounted 90 horsepower outboard engine, leaving his arms free for casting and reeling. A 10 horsepower outboard and an electric trolling motor joined the big engine on the transom, each controlled from the console.

The Laughing Trout

Just forward of Sponzini's perch was a sonar repeater, pedestal mounted, that indicated the presence of fish as well as underwater objects such as sunken trees and shoals.

To his left was a collapsible map pulpit, built like a music stand with clips at top and sides, on which he could place charts. A piece of clear vinyl was fitted over the chart to protect it from spray and fish blood.

In the bottom of the seat forward of Sponzini's perch was a circulating tank in which fish could be kept in ambient water. Many were the bass that had tailed in its water, Sponzini thought smugly. This trout business is really just the same. Organization is the key.

At both stern and bow of the boat were two Danforth anchors, each with a neatly furled line carefully attached to securing eyes.

A twenty-five-foot safety line was attached to an eye welded onto the chair pedestal. At its other end was a clip that Sponzini attached to his belt loop. Finally, for times of rain or hot sun, a canvas top with a clear plastic windshield could be raised forward of the pedestal seat.

The outfitting of this boat had sent a dozen craftsmen and boat workers into fits of frothing indignation as Sponzini insisted on micrometer perfection in selection and placement of all its parts.

Two men had even quit, returning only after Sponzini's project left the shop.

Sponzini stood at the boat ramp on Island Park Reservoir, admiring the boat's fine lines and shiny, waxed aluminum surface as it gently lifted and fell in the light midday breeze.

He had taken two hours to prepare the boat, securing lines, seating, testing, and adjusting its motors—the big engine for running at speed, the trolling motor for slow speed fishing at depth. He calibrated the fish-finder, and packed the boat to be certain of proper weight distribution. After that, he turned to his fishing equipment. He prepared a half-dozen leaders with lures purchased at the Island Park Lodge tackle shop and organized his tackle box for trout, moving all the bass plugs and plastic worms into lidded poly storage bins. The tackle box compartments now shone with Flatfish and Daredevils and SuperDoopers and Hotshots.

He pulled on his day-glo life jacket, carefully securing the clips across his chest, and checked the emergency light to make certain it worked. Then Sponzini untied the bow line and stepped aboard.

He clipped the safety line to his belt and settled onto the pedestal seat, lowering it several clicks to assure himself he was properly perched for running at speed. He placed a blue baseball cap with colonel's scrambled eggs on his head, adjusting it carefully according to the angle of the sun and the wind that would be whipping across his face.

Sponzini clicked the parts of the seatbelt together and looked straight ahead, his nose tilted upward. He reached for the console without looking at it, found the starter button, and stabbed it. The big engine bubbled to life instantly.

Sponzini backed from the ramp moorage slowly.

Pressing his left foot on the turn pedal, he pushed the throttle forward. The boat lifted its bow and shot forward with a growl in a wide, creamy arc, then settled on a pulsing steady course for the far side of Island Park Reservoir.

Sponzini, perched like a dog on the cab of a pickup truck, sniffed and surveyed as the wind took his breath away and sent tiny streamers of tear tracings along his temples from the corners of his eyes.

The rhythmic thump of the boat as it crested the afternoon chop made Herbert Hoover Sponzini feel alive and, well, heroic, he thought, sliding the throttle back as he looked around the lake. It was time to fish. The boat's bow dropped, and it began to bob in the back-wake.

Drawing the six-foot trolling rod with its big, shiny reel from the storage grips on the side of the boat, Sponzini carefully removed the frog Flatfish from its hook protectors and tested the sharpness of its points with his finger tip.

Satisfied, he lowered the lure over the stern of the boat and began feeding out lengths of colored, lead core line, thirty feet per color. About a hundred feet, the tackle shop had suggested. He watched the lure disappear in the green water, glimmering until it was lost to view at a depth of fifteen or twenty feet.

Feeding line, Sponzini reached back and pushed the starter button for the small trolling engine. It sputtered to life and settled into a comforting chug-chug-chug, deemed about right, Sponzini thought, for trolling at depth.

Maybe two or three miles an hour, the man had said.

In less than thirty seconds, the motor revolutions began dropping as the small outboard strained. At the same time, Sponzini felt the steady pull of the line. He looked back at the engine from his seat. The problem was readily apparent: the tough trolling line had wrapped around the propeller shaft. This trolling business would take some getting used to, he thought as he put the little engine in neutral and set the rod in a rod holder.

Sponzini, checking his safety line, moved back to the engine to unravel the trolling line. He lifted the engine out of the water, revealing the small rat's nest of colored line twisted around the motor shaft. He carefully untwisted the line, piling it in the bottom of the boat as each twist was removed.

Once the shaft was clear, Sponzini returned to his seat and reeled in the slack. Now the Flatfish hooks bit into the furled anchor rope as the line moved toward him. He angrily

Whoops

stood up and moved to the back of the boat again where he carefully worked the sharp hooks out of the rope.

With the lure free at last, Sponzini stood up in the transom, braced himself on the little motor, and threw the lure and line behind the boat. This effort coincided with the arrival of the wake of a passing powerboat. It dislodged his braced hand, which struck the manual speed control of the trolling motor. The boat jumped sharply forward and dumped Sponzini unceremoniously backward over the transom and into Island Park Reservoir. He was shocked as he splashed head-first into the cold, green water.

In a moment, he felt himself tugged by the safety line, now stretched taut over the stern, pulling him along behind the boat at a steady walking speed.

The position of the safety clip at the front of his trousers caused him to be pulled head first, then legs first, as he fought to grasp the rope. He gasped as he tried to get hold of the line, only to be rolled head-and-tail by the frothing green water. At last he got a grip by working his hand from his belt to a point several feet up the line. He now held on to it with both hands, his nose splitting the water like the prow of a canoe.

Sponzini briefly felt in control. The stern of the boat was only fifteen feet away. His life jacket kept him afloat. He would pull himself up to the stern and climb on board.

The drag of water against a man is surprisingly powerful when a boat is moving, Sponzini thought. He pulled himself ahead but found it very hard to move even inches against the pull.

Most of the water that fills Island Park Reservoir originates at Big Springs, one of the sources of the Henry's Fork of the Snake River. When it spews forth from the ancient basaltic depths it is about 52 degrees Fahrenheit, and it warms but

The Laughing Trout

little as it is joined by snow-fed tributaries in its five-mile trip to the waters of Island Park Reservoir.

And so it was that Sponzini felt himself getting an erection as he struggled to get to the boat.

It was then he remembered the doctor's admonishment.

Worse, in his struggles with the line, he had caused the motor to turn to one side, which now meant it towed him in a large circle in the center of the lake. Sponzini was frightened—as frightened as ever he had been in Vietnam.

His strength was ebbing, and he could not pull himself up the line against the icy, moving water.

In spite of the loss of dignity, his fear caused him to begin crying out.

"H-H-H-HELP!" came the call, barely heard by the Wixoms, a couple from Twin Falls who were still-fishing a couple of miles away in a small inlet.

Through binoculars they found the source of the calls—a bass boat circling in the center of the lake. It was driverless and seemed to be pulling something. After some discussion, the Wixoms reeled in, started their engine, and putt-putted to the bass boat, warily waiting to snag it as it made one of its passes.

"I don't understand it," Mr. Wixom told Marshal Beal Finnegan at the boat ramp as they poured the limp, blue-lipped, glassy-eyed Sponzini into Beal's vehicle. Sponzini moaned slightly and clutched at his tumescent crotch.

"When we pulled him in he had a hard-on that woulda done a pony proud," Mr. Wixom continued.

"Yes," said Mrs. Wixom. "We could hardly pull him over the side of the boat. It kept catching on it. What do you suppose he was trying to *do* out there?"

CHAPTER TWENTY-NINE

Shocking Spectacle

"What the hell is going on!" shouted Jud Buckalew as his long stride shot him down the slope from his truck.

Suzanne Hsu leaped from the idling truck and raced to catch up with Jud as he approached Mark Bosham, his crew of fish shockers, and assorted bystanders at Last Chance.

Bosham was holding high a fourteen-pound rainbow trout for all to see. Its gills worked ever slower, its jaws gaping for the watery sustenance that had succored it for many years.

"It's the Pig!" said Jud in a high, unearthly voice cracking with rage.

Minutes before the big fish had been shocked to the surface. Bosham was quick to heft it for the benefit of the watching fishermen.

"We'll keep this one," he announced, "for study purposes." Actually Bosham was marveling at how good the fish

The Laughing Trout

would look on his office wall. He'd have to hurry and ice it down to preserve its color and keep it from drying.

Jud burst through the assembled crowd, scattering surprised fishermen. He pulled back his right arm. His swing came from low and behind, gaining power as his fist moved up swiftly, directed at the side of Mark's chin. Bosham had on his best grille grin as he turned in perfect time for Jud's fist to smack into his mouth.

Now the crowd leaped back from the madman in their midst. Jud pulled back his fist for another hit. Blood cascaded over Mark's lower lip. Slowly he fell backward, his arms outspread, the big trout leaving his hand.

Splop, the trout slid into the water. Jud saw it floating belly-up as the current caught it and began tumbling it slowly away, its white underside growing dimmer as it drifted deeper into the river.

In slow motion, Bosham was waving his arms, trying to keep his balance. At last he sat heavily in the river, the green and white water rushing over the tops of his waders.

Instantly he stood up, shrieking and shaking, his broken teeth chattering. *Yeeeeeeeeeee!* It was a wailing cry. He lost his balance and tumbled forward, thrusting his arms into the river.

Yeeeeeeeeeeeeee! he repeated, his eyes rolling wildly as he flailed about trying to stand.

A puzzled Jud on the bank wondered why his blow had caused such peculiar behavior. Now Bosham was doing a strange jumping dance on all fours as he desperately tried to get out of the shallows and on to the bank.

"*Tuuuuurrrrnnn itofff!*" Bosham shouted, looking wild-eyed.

The fish-shocking crew looked on, stunned by the incident and the performance, unconscious of the fact that the

Shocking Spectacle

electrical generator was jolting Bosham at full power. His unprotected, wet skin was completing the circuit.

The spectators were agog at Bosham's novel Snake River Shuffle. Now he was doing a buck-and-wing sideways toward the bank. One arm pointed skyward. His hair was frizzed and erect. His beard stood out on his face like porcupine quills.

Jud caught one last sight of the Pig's white belly as the current rolled the big fish downstream.

"You better turn off the generator," Jud shouted as he took a startled Suzanne by the arm and led her toward the truck.

CHAPTER THIRTY

Mea Culpa

"This phony trout business has gotten out of hand," said a smoldering, shaking Jud, facing Suzanne in the truck.

"Phony trout business?" said Suzanne.

"It has caused too much trouble. It's not fun anymore," said Jud.

"Oh-oh. Do I want to hear this?" said Suzanne suspiciously.

Jud explained simply. Rollo Pasko had attempted to genetically create a trout for Lake Poopo—Lago Poopo—in Bolivia. It started as a practical joke on Bosham.

"If anyone finds out where the fish came from, Rollo will be fired," groaned Jud. "It got out of hand but I didn't dare tell anyone."

"Not even me, Jud?" said Suzanne.

"I'm telling you now."

"You've let me make a fool of myself on national television? You knew better all the time?" Suzanne's eyes welled with tears.

The Laughing Trout

"Wait, this doesn't change things between us. I love you," said Jud, moving toward her. She pushed him away.

"It changes *everything!* I fell in love with you because I trusted your honesty, your vulnerability. I never felt the way I felt about you—ever—with anyone else! It was so right, so real. So instant and so perfect. I gave myself to you unconditionally. And you knew all along that I was making a fool of myself," she said emotionally, slamming the truck door.

"Oh, God, what have I done," Jud despaired. He watched in stunned surprise as Suzanne walked swiftly toward the Laughing Trout, tears rolling down her cheeks.

A wind kicked up, moaning through the pines, riffling the water of the river, bringing clouds to gray the landscape.

CHAPTER THIRTY ONE

Cox's Luck

"Give 'er some goddamn power," shouted Cuss Cox.

Frieda's plump foot dropped on the accelerator and the wheels of the Dodge pickup spun again. Black muck flew back over the boat and trailer. They were stuck in a marshy bog at the edge of Island Park Reservoir. The truck sucked the trailer forward a mere inch through the hub-deep mud.

Cuss was covered with mud. Only the whites of his eyes glared through the brown paste. His chest heaved from the exertion of placing logs, loose sod, and gravel beneath the truck tires to give them traction.

"Wouldna happened if you'd listened," Frieda pointed out. "I told you it looked soft. Your temper gets you in more fixes. We coulda waited for the ramp to get clear … " Frieda pushed her hat back and returned her hands to the steering wheel.

"Shut the shit up," snapped the panting little man, wiping mud from his lips as his teeth ground grit.

The Laughing Trout

In twenty minutes of tire grinding, they'd moved the truck, camper and boat only a dozen feet, leaving a tire-heaved rut from the lake edge through the wet, black marsh.

"Stay in the truck," said Cuss. I'll be back in a few goddamn shittin' minutes."

"I don't want to get out," said Frieda, looking down with distaste at the mud surrounding the truck.

Rulon Cox shuffled away, leaving a trail of sopping black goo on the dirt access road.

An hour later he returned, riding in the back of the Last Chance Tow Truck ("You're not gonna ride in my cab like that," said Beal Finnegan, snapping down the brim of his Smokey Bear hat after Cuss engaged his services).

Frieda saw the tow truck pull up and wondered why Cuss was riding in the back of it. Finnegan got out as Cuss dismounted.

"Here. You're already dirty," said Finnegan, handing Cuss the tow line to hook on the truck.

"Up your ass. Your fee includes hookin' it up!"

Cuss was spitting mad. Finnegan saw he could push the little man only so far.

Finnegan tipped back his Smokey Bear hat and attached the tow line, wincing as the mud sucked at his ankles. He returned to the truck and pulled a lever.

The winch ground out a metallic tune, and the truck and boat slowly pulled forward, making obscene sounds as the mud pulled at the wheels.

"A hundred bucks. Cash, please," said Finnegan as he unhooked the cable.

"You didn't say nothin about goddam cash," roared Cuss.

"Cash. I am the only game in town," said Finnegan with mock humility. "I can winch you back into the mud if you want," he added sweetly. "Or, as marshal, I can impound the car and you can pay the release fee. It's $250. Your choice."

Cuss fumbled through his wallet, grumbling.

"Frieda, I need another forty bucks," he said.

Frieda fished through her floppy woven bag and withdrew her snap-purse. She handed her currency to Cuss.

"That's all the cash I got," she said with finality.

Cuss paid Finnegan. Frieda slid to the passenger side of the cab as Cuss got in, and the tow-truck disappeared in the pines down the road.

"I don't care if I never see this goddamn pissin' place again," said Cuss as he turned the ignition key."*Row-wow ... wow ... ... wow ... .clickclickclick* went the ignition.

The battery was dead.

"Fuck!" screamed Cuss at the top of his lungs, the first time his wife had ever, ever heard him use that word.

"Rulon Cox!" she blurted out and began to cry. Defeated, Cuss put his head on the wheel as scabs of dried mud crumbled into his lap and onto the upholstery of the new Dodge.

For several minutes, the cab was filled only with the sounds of Frieda's sobs and whimpers. Then a light began shining through the fog of adversity as Cuss realized they could soon be on their way, forever leaving Island Park and its miseries.

He remembered the camper had its own 12 volt auto battery to power the electric lights!

Cuss popped the hood of the truck and quickly wrenched off the battery cables. He lifted the battery and carried it to the camper, where he set it on the cushion of the seat of the camper table.

He did not see the truck battery slowly topple against the chrome strip of the table and make a connection. He was too busy disconnecting the camper battery to see the wisp of smoke.

"What a pissin' mess this turned out to be," he grumbled as he slammed the camper door and turned to install the battery under the hood of the truck.

"Let's go," he snapped as he climbed back into the truck, smearing grease from his hands alongside the mud on the upholstered seat.

Frieda sniffled and dabbed at her eyes with her handkerchief. The ordeal appeared to be over.

The truck started with a roar. Cuss now remembered the problems with the electrical circuits they had fought on the way up. By God, this truck would go back to the dealer tomorrow. And he would make 'em keep it until everything was goddamn pissin' perfect. There were lemon laws ...

"Do you smell smoke?" said Frieda.

"Naw," said Cuss, watching the speedometer hit seventy as the truck and trailer rolled down the long hill from Island Park toward Ashton.

The trees rushed by. The white lines of the highway shot beneath them.

As the highway widened to four lanes, a sedan with Idaho plates drew alongside, honking and pointing back at the camper.

"I *know* I smell smoke," said Frieda ominously as Cuss stared at the sedan.

Cuss drew to a stop. They got out. Great billows of smoke and fingers of flame roared from the rear of the camper. Cuss tried to shield his face from the flames and opened the camper door.

A great burst of fire belched from the open door and knocked him to the asphalt, torching his eyebrows off and burning his hair back to his crown.

"That was a big mistake," he muttered, patting at the wisps of smoldering hair and clothing. The battery had caught the drapes on fire; the drapes had burned through the propane line. The propane was roaring like a blowtorch.

"Save the boat!" shouted Frieda.

Cuss tried to get close enough to unhook the trailer and boat. The devil himself couldn't stand the heat.

In the next hour, they helplessly learned that even metal campers burn intensely.

They watched the lashing flames turn their new Dodge truck into a black and smoking shell, standing like a war casualty on tireless black rims in smoldering puddles of melted rubber and asphalt.

Cuss and Frieda also learned that aluminum boats—at certain temperatures—melt like beer cans, and that volunteer, small-town fire departments take a long time to respond.

Nothing was saved.

CHAPTER THIRTY-TWO

Good Plan

"I'm in deep shit," sighed Gordon Okleberry, looking at his gnarled farm-worked hands as they clutched his glass. They were two days overdue. There was no Bosham trout. No trout at all, for that matter.

Max Dodick sipped a vermouthless martini. Gin was the only liquor left in Vera's depleted stock. Vera splashed in a little peach flavored wine cooler for body.

Max was thinking. Bev would be spitting bullets when he got home. It would be ugly. Things might get thrown.

Okleberry's thoughts were on his wife, too. "Judy's threatened to leave before, you know," said Okleberry. Once, she'd gone out and bought a spa membership and a set of china out of anger at his being drunk. She was capable of *anything*.

"Never happen. We'll think of something," said the implement salesman, knocking back the last of his drink with a grimace.

The Laughing Trout

Weaving, they made their way to their car. In turn, it weaved out onto the highway.

It was after they passed the burning truck and trailer ("Hell! Look at that boat melt!") that Max had The Great Idea.

"Look, Gordie. If they thought we were hurt or something, then they wouldn't get mad, right?"

"Right. I guess," said the drooping farmer, still trying to make sense of a boat burning at the side of a four-lane blacktop highway.

Dodick turned from the steering wheel and said, conspiratorially: "We'll make 'em think one of us got hurt."

The car drifted onto the shoulder. He corrected, sending the vehicle swerving madly before straightening out.

"It may be a self-fulfilling prophecy," said Okleberry, "Watch the road."

"Now, listen," said Dodick. "When we get to St. Anthony, I'll take your car and you take mine. Then when you get home you tell your wife *I* got sick and you had to take me to the hospital. Then I'll tell my wife *you* got sick and I had to take you to emergency. It's perfect!

We got each other's car to prove it!"

"Oh. I get it." It did seem very clever to Okleberry. Sometimes that Max really was a whizbang.

With Dodick's car, his wife would definitely be disarmed.

"Max, you're a genius."

Day Eighteen
San Francisco

CHAPTER THIRTY-THREE

At NBC

Soft, rounded furniture in grays and mauves reflected the blue glow of the bank of television monitors. Michael Goff settled back into a chair to await the footage from Suzanne Hsu in faraway Idaho. To get a live shot, they'd sent a truck with an uplink from the Snake River, which in turn fed the NBC affiliate in Idaho Falls for re-transmission.

The zig-zag of lines snapped into a picture and Suzanne looked out from the screen, wetting her lips, pushing her hair back. Goff absently plucked at the arm of the chair; Suzanne's image reminded him of how much he missed her. God, just that one night, he recalled with longing.

"Is the downlink clean yet?" he asked, depressing the button on the dull silver microphone that rose like a snake next to the console.

"Ready," said a loudspeaker.

"Ready," said Suzanne on the monitor.

The Laughing Trout

She does not look telegenic tonight, Mike thought. "Hold it," he said into the mike. "Suzanne. Are you okay?"

"I'm okay," she said sharply.

Michael Goff waited before responding. "Loosen up, Suzanne. This is a light, fluffy confection of a story."

"It's a bullshit story, Michael," said Suzanne. Michael was always startled when the face on the monitor cursed; his years in television consisted of thousands of oily, unctuous, sanctimonious, purified deliveries. Any profanity was forbidden, due to the slight chance it could get aired.

"Suzanne," he said, a whine of warning in his voice, "you know the network rules—"

"Let's get this done," she said abruptly.

"THREE, TWO, ONE," announced the monitor.

Suzanne smiled sardonically and began speaking, the distant Tetons looming over her shoulder, the sound of the Snake River growling gently in the background. "Fishermen since the time of Izaak Walton have been accused of exaggeration, if not outright lies. It's traditional in the sport. And up here in Idaho, noses have been growing longer than the fish. Pinocchio-style noses, that is.

"For the past few days the silly season has brought trout frenzy to this corner of southeastern Idaho, where droves of fishermen have come in an attempt to catch an alleged new species of trout carrying a fifty thousand dollar reward for its live capture.

"Well, it turns out it's all a hoax. NBC today learned that what started as a private joke got out of hand."

Suzanne's face was replaced by footage of Bosham holding the trout. Bosham was ponderously explaining the nature of fangs, the pectorals, and the tiny eyes.

"This is a new species," said Bosham seriously.

The face of Suzanne was back on the monitor. "Definitely NOT a new species," she said into the camera. "Instead the

At NBC

fish is believed to have been a genetically engineered mistake. A booboo. A glitch. The fish was part of an experiment being conducted by the U.S. State Department in cooperation with the U. S. Fish and Wildlife Service's Fisheries Research Laboratory."

The camera was back on the trout. Suzanne was speaking voice-over.

"The trout was part of the State Department's economic development program for third world countries. It was being bred in order to start a fishery for Bolivia in the country's Lake Poopo. Yes, that's a real lake in Bolivia."

Suzanne was back on camera, the river flowing between piney banks behind her.

"But something went wrong. The result was the bizarre trout that found its way to Idaho to fool both experts and fishermen, the practical joke by one of the local guides which had everyone making fools of themselves. "The only winners: the local businesses that have sold out of supplies and every conceivable kind of alcohol. Trout insanity ... comes to an end in Idaho. Suzanne Hsu, NBC News, Island Park, Idaho."

Her face with its fixed end-of-story hint of a smile lingered on-screen.

"CUT," said the loudspeaker. Suzanne relaxed. "Sorry Michael," she said, looking out from the monitor. "I know that's not what you expected, but we are in the business of truth, are we not?" Suzanne started wrapping up the mike cord.

Michael plucked at the chair arm for a few moments.

"Suzanne," he said, flicking the mike switch. He paused.

"Suzanne. It's a great story. A terrific end. But I want you to make some changes. Get some shots of people leaving. Get some interviews with them. Can you get that guy Bosham? And can you find the guys who perpetrated the hoax? Show me the empty shelves of the stores and the litter from the crowds. You know, the end-of-the-game kind of story—"

Suzanne peered quizzically from the monitor, a smile breaking on her face.

"Yeah. I can get that. You'll have to get Washington to sleuth out one of the perpetrators. He's in Maryland. His name is Rollo Pasko. I'll see what I can do about getting the local jokers."

Day Eighteen
Island Park

CHAPTER THIRTY-FOUR

Vera's Mission

Vera Segura had six burgers, eight beers, a grilled cheese, and a bowl of chili in various stages of preparation when she heard the phone ringing above the chatter in the bar. She wiped her hands on the spattered and smeared apron that girdled her. She lifted the phone.

"It's me, Beal, and I need your he'p," he said.

Vera heard a pleading note from the town marshal.

"Now what?" she said breathlessly. "These last few days have been the goofiest … "

"This is serious. I got a man up here who nearly drowned in Island Park Reservoir, needs the hospital, or maybe a whorehouse," Beal added with a snicker. Vera was curious, but let Finnegan continue.

"Then I got a kid who was freakin' out all the folks at Coffee Pot Rapids, needs a jail cell. Then I got a call from Forest Service 'n' they tell me a couple's rig is all a'fire down on Highway 20 below Riverside.

The Laughing Trout

Meanwhile, there's a traffic jam at Mack's Inn and people are gettin' *ugly*. I should be up there," he concluded.

"So what can I do?" said Vera with a sigh. It was true. The Bosham trout business had turned Island Park into a nuthouse.

"Will you drive the soaker to the hospital and the kid to the jail in your van? I think we can rig a litter up so the Eyetalian's comfortable—he's the soaker.

The kid is jest kind of, well, weird. Harmless, I think.

I can cuff him to the seat," said Beal.

Vera calculated the driving time to Rexburg and back: two hours, maybe more depending on traffic and contingencies at the hospital and jail.

"Okay," she said. "Bring 'em over. We'll work it out."

She held down the phone receiver and then lifted it again. She would have to call in Mort to watch the bar.

Twenty minutes later, she heard car tires crunching in the gravel. She knew it was Beal: she could see his whippy antenna jiggling through the small kitchen window as she dished up an order of tacos.

Beal and Laramie Mort clomped into the cool darkness of the bar together, and Mort pulled on an apron, relieving Vera.

Vera fluffed her hair and looked in her hand mirror as they walked to Beal's car.

As she looked inside, she was surprised to see the glazed eyes and slowly moving lips of her cabin guest, Sponzini. He lay up against the corner of the rear seat, groaning, his usually immaculate black hair creeping across his cheeks in wet points and wisps.

On the other side of the back seat sat young Christopher Cochran, singing to himself in bored resignation.

"What's the deal with Mr. Sponzini? " she said.

Beal moved back a few paces so as not to be heard.

Vera's Mission

"Well, he's got a hard-on that won't go away. I called the emergency at Rexburg. Told them this guy Sponzini had been accidentally dragged around the reservoir by his boat. He had been in the water for twenty minutes, anyway. So his teeth was just a chatterin' away when they got to him. That water's so cold, you know. Anyways, the EMTs ask if he's on any medications. I ask him. He can barely talk, but says yes, he's taking something called, like, Terpentine, or Peppermine.

Anyways, the EMTs knew what it was, and it seems like the cold water reacts with the medicine and bingo, the guy's got a throbber the size of a fish whacker.

They call it a priapism. *Priapism*," Beal repeated with satisfaction. "Means his dink is gonna be wavin' for a while, at least," he snickered.

Vera's eyes and mouth were wide as she listened.

She moved closer. Sure enough, the blankets protruded over Sponzini's crotch like a teepee.

"Anything you can give him?" she said.

"The docs in Rexburg told me to give him a shot of Demerol from my medicine kit to ease his pain, which I did. Priapism hurts, they told me. Now Mr. Sponzini is started to hallucinate on the Demerol, I guess. Keeps repeating his ailment. Priapism, priapism, like that.

Then his teeth chatter like a rattler," said Beal, now opening the trunk of his car. He removed a collapsible litter and began snapping it together.

Vera opened the rear doors of the van. If they placed the litter over the tops of the bench seats it would ride there comfortably and safely. With the help of Vera's customers, they soon had Sponzini laid out flat on the litter as they carefully inserted him into the van. Beal lashed the litter down with lengths of bungie cord to keep it from bouncing or shifting,

The Laughing Trout

then lashed Sponzini on the litter with two more lengths for good measure.

"Priapism," moaned Sponzini, his voice low. "Priapism," he said, his voice rising. He drew the word out loudly, his eyes half-shut, his head rolling from side to side. The small mountain in his crotch was aimed at the overhead light.

Finnegan now unlocked Cochran and led him to the van.

"'Lo," Cochran said cheerily to Vera, as Finnegan clicked the handcuff chain to the runner of the backseat.

"How do," said Vera. He was just a kid, a high-school acne case with hippie hair.

"You might check out that rig that burned up down by Riverside. Firemen should have it out by now. I'll just have to get to it when I can," said Finnegan, shaking his head as he pushed the van door closed.

Beal Finnegan gave Vera the key to the cuffs and yelled after her as she gingerly pulled onto Highway 20: "When you turn him over to the jailer, don't forget to get my cuffs back!"

Past the Railroad Ranch, the van moved south on the blacktop, swirling the stands of roadside fireweed in its windstream. Vera glanced through the rearview mirror.

Sponzini was rolling his head slowly now, only occasionally voicing the litany of his ailment. The teepee still proudly stood in his crotch, Vera noted its magnificence with a soft rush of air from her lungs.

The lodgepole pines whipped past, then gave way to undulating lands with stumps and shattered timber, the war zone of ongoing clear-cut timbering.

Cochran was absently looking out the window, one arm hanging down, locked onto the seat. He seemed to be singing opera, but she was not certain over the grind of the engine. She shifted down as the van started up the hill north of Riverside. Clearing the top, the highway straightened and widened into four lanes. She saw a curl of greasy smoke above the pines.

Slowing, Vera pulled closer to the smoke at the roadside. She came to a halt at the smoldering wreckage.

A small pumper truck from the town of Ashton dribbled a stream of water on the skeletal remains of the Cox's truck, camper, and boat.

"Jeeeesus, that was a mistake," intoned Cuss Cox for the fiftieth time, delicately fingering his cheeks and nose. He sat on a blanket on the ground. Most of his face was sooty black. His eyebrows, eyelashes were singed completely off, and he smelled of burnt hair.

Frieda, looking fresh and pale as an uncooked sausage beneath her broad-brimmed gardening hat, had borrowed Noxema from a sympathetic bystander and was dabbing the white paste on the pink spots on Cuss's nose and brow where the blaze had blistered the skin.

"You better come with me, folks," said Vera gently, surveying the little man's face. "I'm headed for the hospital in Rexburg."

He needed first aid and maybe more, judging by the insane look in his eyes, she thought.

She helped Cuss and Frieda into the van. Frieda fussed and clucked, picking at her man solicitously. "'Lo," said Cochran, his eyes wide with awe at the wreckage and its survivors.

"Priapism," moaned Sponzini.

"What's he say? What's he say?" asked the agitated Cuss.

"We're taking him to the hospital," volunteered Cochran as Vera rounded the front of the truck to get into the driver's seat.

"Everybody buckled up?" she asked, starting the van.

"I sure am," answered Cochran merrily, lifting his manacled arm.

The van pulled back on the highway for its final leg to Rexburg.

CHAPTER THIRTY-FIVE

The News at Seven

Jud Buckalew desperately wanted a whisky. He sat at Vera's bar watching the evening anchor explain the president's side trip to Lyon from the economic summit in Paris. Jud knew his face would soon be on NBC-TV. Not his voice. Just his face.

In a world gone instantly mad, Lulu Dexter and Don Pellegrini, his friends of the day before, had attacked him with whirring audio-video gear under the aggressive field marshaling of Suzanne Hsu, his lover of the day before.

That very afternoon, he had slipped away from them as they approached his cabin. He had spent the afternoon with a book, hiding in the aspen near Elk Creek where they were unable to find him for an interview. But he was sure they got Sasquatch footage of him as he left his cabin. When he crept back, he learned they had gone with the uplink truck to Idaho Falls.

The Laughing Trout

"I wanna drink, Mort," he said timidly as he entered the bar at 6:59 p.m., a minute before NBC News air time. He had to know what the television would say.

"Where's Vera?" he asked, hoping for solace and information.

"Gone to Rexburg, taking some folks to the hospital in the van. Oh, yeah. And a kid to the jail. A mischief-maker brought by the rush for Mr. Bosham's trout, I guess," said Laramie Mort as he stacked coffee cups still hot from the dishwasher. He looked at Jud levelly.

"You don't really want a drink, Jud."

"I really do, Mort."

"You can't have a drink, Jud," said Mort, crossing his arms over his leather vest and checkered shirt. "There's not an ounce of whiskey or a pony of beer in all of Fremont County, Idaho. I'm sure the trucks are rushing new supplies. But they ain't here yet." He slid open the backbar and the cooler to reveal dark wells of emptiness. Instead, Laramie Mort poured Jud a cup of fresh brewed coffee.

Jud pondered the irony of it; the fates were interfering. A higher power had stepped in. Getting drunk would only make things worse. And Jud could never be sure when he might sober up again.

He was jarred as Suzanne appeared on the bar's TV screen. She was followed by a shot of Bosham's trout.

Then Mark came on, smiling grimly, saying, "They sure had us fooled." And a moment later, he added, "It's amazing what we are able to do with bioengineering these days. It has much promise for the future of the fisheries professionals."

Jud shook his head in disbelief, marveling at the Mark's boundless ability to twist and turn through the rocks and reefs of reality like a snake through a bed of prickly pear.

Then there was video footage of Jud. He winced.

The News at Seven

" ... the perpetrator, a local guide ... " was all he heard.

He watched himself turn from the camera. There was an edit. Three seconds of film. Nothing more.

" ... aided by Rollo Pasko, a former U.S. Fish and Wildlife Service fisheries biologist and manager ... " said Suzanne's voice.

"*Former!* Let the wild beasts scatter my bones," wailed Jud. He was too convulsed with anguish to pay attention to the local news when it came on. But Mort's attention was pulled to the set by the sound of a band attempting to play "Somewhere, Over the Rainbow." The camera was over panning the red and white uniforms, tall hats and spatted feet of young band members. REXBURG H.S. BAND, announced a banner as the camera cut away from it, then went close-up on three puffy-blond teenage girls imitating percherons as they high-stepped smartly forward, their batons flashing like scimitars in the early evening light.

"Hellooo, eastern Idaho!" said a smiling, smoothly-coifed television announcer as his face was superimposed over the strutting majorettes. "Welcome to the annual Route 20 Festival, live from Rexburg. I'm Bret Douglas, and I'm here with most of the town as eastern Idaho gets ready to meet, greet, and gift the one millionth vehicle traveling scenic Route 20 this year in the fabulous country of Island Park and Yellowstone."

The camera slowly moved across faces of the assembled community, reducing them to the appearance of tightly packed confetti on the screen. The band played—or tried to play—"Captain from Castile." The sousaphone was a half-beat behind, and the trumpets could not reach the high notes.

A valiant effort, thought Mort, wiping a glass, looking at the mournful Jud Buckalew who sat shaking his head, staring into his untouched coffee.

The Laughing Trout

The announcer on TV was joined by another talking head.

"Folks, Rexburg Mayor Garth Phibbs is going to tell us why this festival is so important, and how it works. Mayor?"

"Thank you, Bret," said the genial head with freckles, big ears, and russet hair.

"You know, all this began during my first term as mayor when I suggested that we commemorate the traffic on Route 20 that brings tourist dollars and jobs to our area of eastern Idaho. With a group of like-minded citizens we decided that to hold the Route 20 Festival would not only give thanks to our tourists, but would also get us more publicity and make the community aware of how important development is to our well-being," he droned on, his vowels flattened by years of isolation in southeastern Idaho's Mormon farm culture.

Bump-bump-bump-da-da-bump, went the drums in the background. A banshee's wail went up from the clarinet section. People shuffled as the camera panned up and down the highway lined by the assembled crowd.

"Now, the next vehicle you see will be the one millionth car to travel Route 20 this year," explained the mayor. "Each year we set our counter January first, and by summer we estimate we reach one million. Right now our counter says 999,999, so the next car you folks see will be the big one, and boy! will they be surprised," Mayor Phibbs squealed.

Looking south, the camera saw nothing on the highway. The camera took a telephoto shot north up the highway, past the turn-of-the-century Rexburg Co-op Building, past the Cenex Tower, past the Texaco. A blue vehicle appeared as a dot in the center of the screen. "Here they come, folks," said the announcer.

The News at Seven

"An exciting moment," assured the mayor.

The vehicle drew closer, slowing hesitantly.

"It's a van, folks," said the mayor. "And it has Idaho plates, so it's one of our own. And you know, if Idahoans will vacation in Idaho, that means the dollars stay here," the mayor added.

"What does it say on the front of the van, Mayor?" asked the announcer.

The camera moved close-up on the front of the van: YENROH ER'UOY FI KNOH, it read.

"Yenroh, ah, eroy, ah, fi ... they must be foreign-speaking Idahoans, Bret. Basque or Finnish, perhaps," said the Mayor, trying to pronounce the writing on the bug screen of the Van.

"Holy shit, it's Vera!" exclaimed Laramie Mort from behind the bar.

Jud looked up at the screen. It was indeed Vera with her ragged group of survivors.

The van rolled to a stop as the band, the officials, and the TV camera converged on it. Jud and Laramie Mort could see Vera's eyes, wide and bright, as she tugged at her hair with a comb.

The announcer and mayor worked through the band, now playing what might have been the theme from *Star Wars*, and thrust a microphone at Vera as they opened the doors of the van.

Vera looked around with alternating smiles and fearful looks.

"Congratulations, and welcome to the Route 20 Festival," said the mayor over the sound the band.

"The what?" said Vera, cupping her hand to her ear.

"The ROUTE 20 FESTIVAL," shouted the mayor. "Did you say *RIOT* FESTIVAL?" said Vera, confused and deafened.

The Laughing Trout

Suddenly Christopher Cochran's head appeared in the television frame.

"He said *RAT FESTIVAL*. Isn't that great! A celebration of man's true accomplishment for the environment. Everywhere man's gone, he's brought the *RAT!*" squealed Cochran with delight, jerked back to his seat by the handcuff as he tried to push closer to the camera and microphone.

Cochran motioned the microphone closer: "And if this is a RAT 20 FESTIVAL, imagine what a RAT 50 FESTIVAL would be folks!"

Sensing something amiss, the mayor and announcer returned to Vera.

Now preened and composed, Vera offered her name and said: "I am delighted to be here and part of this great celebration."

A relieved mayor and announcer pressed on as it became apparent that the driver of the millionth vehicle was enjoying her fling with fame.

"What brings you down Route 20 to Rexburg today?" asked the announcer.

"We had some minor problems ... "

"Minor, my ass," came the muted oath from the small man sitting in a rear seat.

" ... and we're taking these folks to your hospital," Vera continued, not missing a beat, glowing with camera presence.

"We're sorry to hear that," said the mayor, "but we'd like to say hello to the people you have with you today." The camera lens pushed inside the van. "Hi, folks, from all of us in Rexburg, Idaho!" came the announcer's voice.

The camera revealed a small man with no eyebrows and a black and red face. He looked up like a weasel about to lunge at its captor.

The News at Seven

Christopher Cochran lifted his manacled arm, offering a clanking wave for the camera.

"Priapism ... priapism ... PRI-AP-ISM!" shouted the delirious Sponzini as the camera lingered on the teepee in his crotch.

In the bar, Jud and Laramie Mort were now riveted to the television screen, eyes and mouths wide.

The camera pulled back.

"As the one millionth vehicle, you'll get some wonderful prizes from the merchants and businessmen in southeastern Idaho, including a full week's vacation for every one of you at beautiful Island Park," said the mayor.

"Fuck that for sure," said the sooty-faced little man with no eyebrows, looking directly into the camera. The television station cut to a commercial without comment, as if stupefied by what had just been broadcast.

The commercial was followed by regular programming, in this case a re-run of "M.A.S.H." Folks were shown no more of the festival doings that evening. A few treasured the videos they had made of those moments, and duplicates became collectors' items.

The mayor, the announcer, and the television station made an on-air apology to the citizens of eastern Idaho for "the obscenities that may have offended our community."

Thirty minutes later, Vera unloaded her ragged band at the Rexburg Community Hospital. She left Cochran manacled in the van but returned with a magazine for him to read while he waited.

Sponzini was carried in on his litter, answering "priapism" when the nurse asked for his name. The Coxes slumped in chairs awaiting their turn with the doctor, who was already busy with two patients, brought just a few minutes before by a Fremont County deputy sheriff.

The Laughing Trout

The nurses clucked professionally over Sponzini's tumescent member.

The tall, crew-cut deputy ambled out of the emergency room, writing on his clipboard. He turned to the gathered group and officially said: "Doc will be a few minutes. We'll get you right into E.R."

Vera surmised she might get the deputy to take Cochran off her hands and save her a trip to the jail. "Deputy," she began, "would you by any chance be headed for the jail? I have a boy our marshal arrested who I've been instructed to turn over to Fremont County."

"I am going to the jail from here. But I've got two dingbats to take already," he said, motioning toward the emergency room with his thumb.

"This kid's not making any trouble, really," she added.

"Maybe I can squeeze him in with the other two. What happened?"

"He was harassing fishermen," she said, passing Finnegan's arrest sheet to the deputy.

He looked at it.

"Island Park, huh? What's going on up there? The place must be bedlam. So far as I've been able to learn, my two clowns in there," he motioned with his thumb toward the E.R. again, "had been in Island Park before their accident."

"It's all gone crazy since they announced the reward for that new trout. What happened with your two?"

Vera asked.

The deputy's eyes rolled up in his head as he began:

"These two drunks are driving toward their respective homes across the flat, treeless, open farmlands north of here. You can see fifty miles in all directions. They're the only cars on the road. What happens?

The News at Seven

They *collide* at the intersection of Teller Road and County 18! Bam! And get this: each is for some reason *driving the other's car!* Can you beat that?" the deputy's dark glasses drooped low on his nose, as he shook his head.

A moment later, the deputy took the two men into custody as they emerged limping and bandaged from the emergency room. Vera recognized them, Dodick and Okleberry, recent habitués of her bar, depletors of the last of her gin.

Day Fifty
Island Park

CHAPTER THIRTY-SIX

Facing Rollo and Other Things

The heat of July settled like a lid on a stew over Island Park.

Smoke boiled from a distant fire in the Targhee; the drone of firefighting bombers soothed Jud in a strange, melancholy way as he strode from his pickup into Vera's.

Jud had a yen for a hamburger and a bundle of Vera's greasy french fries. The brie-and-cracotte days of guiding fisherfolks with fancy tastes left him ready to puke at the sight of cursive French labels.

"How's trips?" said Vera as she slid coffee down the counter to Jud. The bar was host to six or seven dude fishermen wrapping up the day's flailings.

"Pretty good," said Jud. Vera nodded. The flow of visiting fishermen had dropped off dramatically immediately after the Great Hoax, but within a week it had strangely come up again, this time consisting not of reward-seeking

The Laughing Trout

opportunists, but of serious fly fishermen who had been waiting until the Island Park insanity waned and left the river and its trout to calm themselves.

After the Lago Poopo Trout affair was on television, Jud became wary of appearing in public. He feared the people of Island Park would blame him for the madness. He cancelled his trips, packed gear and his cat into the pickup, and drove into the Wind River Mountains where he licked his wounds, never once looking at a fishing rod. He spent his time wandering through the cirques, lying in fields of lupine and bluebells, watching the flat-bottomed clouds boiling over Gannett Peak.

One night as he fished a baked potato out of the coals of his campfire, he realized he must return to Island Park and face his friends, his business, and his future. To remain in the Winds longer was a kind of cowardly escape.

He had been picking at his wounds by reminding himself how stupid he had been: Jud Buckalew, the man who lost forever $9,400 hard-earned dollars and his beloved wife and all their dreams with it. He could blame that on booze. But what about sober Jud Buckalew, the man who hurt Rollo Pasko, a long time friend? And his most acute question, what about Suzanne Hsu?

"What ifs," "should haves," and "could haves" had troubled Jud's Wind River sleep each night until long after Orion spilled beyond the edge of the world.

First, he tried to bury all thought of the events.

Then he remembered: "We are only as sick as our innermost secrets," and "Don't forget to forgive yourself."

Time to return. Time to learn that even bad experiences can be good teachers. He had not taken that drink.

That was progress. Get going, get back into life. Quit isolating.

Facing Rollo and Other Things

Jud needed to make amends to Rollo and to apologize even to Mark. That would make him feel better.

But how could he apologize to a beautiful big fish whose death he had caused? As for all the people who rushed to Island Park as a result of his hoax, did Jud need to apologize to them? Or were they victims of their own greed? He would meditate on some questions. Jud broke open the fire-roasted potato and chewed its hot, fragrant flesh. Sipping the night-chilled spring water in his canteen, he leaned back on his sleeping bag and prodded the fire, sending sparklets whirl-winding into the Pleiades. Bob the cat kneaded the sleeping bag until at last satisfied it met his standards, then spiraled into its fabric and began to purr like distant thunder.

As he slid into the silken-cold of the sleeping bag, it struck Jud that a simple life had given him pleasure before, and would again. How ridiculously beautiful the Milky Way looks tonight, Jud thought as warmth and sleep enveloped him, so bold and thick, like a stripe of stars painted across the night sky.

The next morning Jud moved down the trail as the first stilettos of sunlight appeared over the shoulder of the peak. The wetness of wyethia darkened his khakis to the knees as he walked through the mountain meadows, led triumphantly by a damp black cat.

The burger and fries brought Jud back to the moment. He chewed slowly, thinking he needed to tie up some micro-caddies and some rusty spinners. He would do that this evening.

Vera picked up her ringing phone. "It's for you," she said, poking her head around the corner of the grill.

"Me? Who the hell could that be?"

The Laughing Trout

Jud tried to swallow a bite of burger to clear his mouth. "Hello?"

"Jud? Pasko here. I tried your cabin and when I couldn't reach you I just knew you would be in a bar. And probably the bar where I sent the Lago Poopo trout." Rollo's laugh was like a nail being pulled from a board.

"Oh, God, Rollo, I've been thinking to call you. I just hadn't worked up the courage."

"Jeezus, your practical joke turned out to be the Chicago Fire," Rollo said chuckling.

"I'm truly sorry I lost you your job," said Jud humbly.

"You did me a favor. I got a new job. A better job."

This was news. Jud felt a little lighter. Rollo was the same old Rollo, not some angry new edition. "Actually," said Rollo, "it was hilarious watching your idiot cousin on national TV. Especially his graceful recovery from a fall that should have assured him certain death. When he said it was a real good joke, it saved his ass.

"Maybe all our asses. The guy has a real talent for bullshit. He's a blow-hard egomaniac. Promoters like him are hard to find in the fish business. That's why I am going to use him in my new position," said Rollo.

"What are you going to be doing?" said Jud. His mind was alert to the nuances and possibilities. Pasko's ironic cackle popped against Jud's ear. "I've accepted the post as director of fisheries for Idaho Fish and Game. They forgave my past indiscretions up at Hell Roaring because they need somebody with my research background. Besides, the commissioners thought it was just about the best practical joke they'd ever heard of. I'm in Boise now. Amazing, isn't it, how things come full circle?"

The announcement stunned Jud speechless.

Pasko continued: "I plan to pull Bosham from the field and put him in as legislative liaison. His bullshit and ability to twist and turn make him an ideal lobbyist. And besides, he'll be right at home with the legislature. They're his kind.

"Now listen closely: I want the best ichthyologist in the business to take over in Island Park. It's one of the primo assignments in Idaho," said Rollo.

"Who's it gonna be?" asked Jud, still on the ceiling from Rollo's announcement, yet aware of the impact that it could have on his business and fishing in the park in general.

"You. I've got it all fixed. You can have it tomorrow. You are as good as they get in the trout business. You can jump-start your career and pick up where you left off."

Jud reeled, sucking in his breath.

"Rollo. Wow. You honor me. Thanks so much, but I've got to think about this. My circuits are easily overloaded, you know. I need some time."

"You have twenty-four hours. I really want you to do this. I'll call you tomorrow night."

Jud hung up the phone, his mind a-flutter.

"I got a nice phone call this morning, too," said the eavesdropping Vera coyly, looking down at the bar top as she polished it.

"Yeah?" said Jud distractedly, Rollo's announcements caroming through his mind.

"Yeah. Colonel Sponzini called from Houston this morning to thank me for helping him and for visiting him in the hospital. Said he'd been here on earth for 20,052 days and realized he had not really been alive until he came close to death—and met me. He says it made him understand what he's missed. He's sending me airline tickets. He's taking me bass fishing in Louisiana after Labor Day. Isn't that nice?" she said, dreamily polishing the bar.

CHAPTER THIRTY-SEVEN

Decisions

Jud waited for Rollo's phone call. He twisted deer hair around a size twenty hook and tied it off. Below, the river rolled in thick, green folds as the shadows deepened. He could see the snout of a good trout rise to slurp the surface three feet from the grassy bank. Nice, a two or three pounder, thought Jud. In fifteen more years it might go ten pounds.

The phone rang.

"Hi, Rollo," said Jud. This was going to be difficult.

"What's the decision, Juddy?" asked Rollo, getting right to the point.

"The decision is a very grateful, thankful, no thank you. It's a tough decision, Rollo. You flatter me. You return to me some lost dignity that I badly needed to have back. But I just can't jump back into the mad milieu of government and the inability to do what's right for the resource because of politics. It was hard on me before. Helped contribute to my personal confusion. Today I'm healthy and generally happy and

The Laughing Trout

I intend to keep myself that way. I've gotta do what's best for me," said Jud.

"I was afraid you'd become too comfortable to put up with the bureaucrats. I knew it was a long shot when I made the offer. But I want you to know it was a sincere offer. And I really plan to do some interesting things with the department," said Rollo seriously. "There's always a place for you as long as I am here," he added gently.

"You're a good guy in my book."

"I might shed a tear if you keep that up," said Jud.

"So you'll just go on guiding dudes?" asked Rollo."

"Yep. Might also put out a newsletter on fishing in the area. I could write feature stories in winter, then plug in the weekly news as it happens. Where the trout are, what they're taking, when they're taking it.

"Fill it with humor and bullshit. That's the nice thing about fishing. Everybody expects a lot of bullshit."

"My God, you *are* learning," roared Rollo.

CHAPTER THIRTY-EIGHT

Maybe

The river was now green-black. A flame of brilliant orange seared the western sky. Little puffs of pink cloud stood high overhead as Jud looked up from the porch chair. Bob was heavy in his lap, purring like a power drill at idle.

Jud was mildly irritated by the sound of the phone from within the cabin. Bob thumped from his lap to the deck as Jud stood.

"Yep," he said instead of hello.

There was silence for several long seconds.

"Jud. It's me. Suzanne."

"Oh. Hi." He spoke shyly, hesitantly.

"You angry at me?" she said tentatively.

"I dunno what I am. Confused, maybe. I figured you were sore at me," Jud said.

"No. Not anymore. I miss you. A lot."

"I miss you, Suzanne," Jud said.

"Do we have any chance at all?"

The Laughing Trout

Another silence.

"I don't know," Jud finally said. "I think about you constantly, whatever that means."

Another long pause.

"I love you, Jud. I think about you every minute."

"Where are you?" Jud said.

"In Washington. I caught the gold ring. But I don't have you."

"You're in D.C. I'm in Idaho. How could it work?"

"I get a lot of time off in summer, when Washington closes shop. You get a lot of time off in winter. Maybe we could make things fit," said Suzanne.

Jud's thoughts were whirling and excited.

"Maybe," he said at last. "But we're from two different worlds. Let's think about it."

"Opposites attract, Jud, my darling. I'll be in Oregon on assignment next week. I could come over to Island Park for a long weekend. What do you say?"

"I say hurry, next week. I might even cancel a couple of bookings."

CHAPTER THIRTY NINE

Epilogue

Bob swaggered through the overhang of deep grass and delicate sego lilies on the north bank of the Snake.

He softly leaped to the top rail of the buck-and-pole fence that marked the edge of the Railroad Ranch. His stomach was round and full of fat, fresh-caught vole. Stretched along the sunny rail full length, he looked up-river to the distant buildings at Last Chance.

His cat eyes watched figures come and go at Vera's. A drift boat pulled into shore, the sound of clunking oars reaching him several seconds after the withdrawn blades flashed in the morning light.

The cat's gaze locked on a great blue heron flying almost on the river surface. The bird's long legs trailed behind him, nearly touching the river as the bird's trajectory dipped with each upstroke of its wings. As the heron passed, something on the surface of the water caught the cat's eye.

The Laughing Trout

From the river rose a great snout clamped onto struggling seven-inch whitefish.

Cat eye met fish eye. The fish eye was the color of a pearl and as big as a quarter. For a moment, a mighty dorsal fin broke the surface, only to be reclaimed by the enveloping waters. Bob's eyes closed slowly as he dozed in the Island Park sun.

###

Epilogue

Jim Ure is a fly fisherman who is frequently found on the Henry's Fork of the Snake River.

Books by Jim Ure (also writing as James W. Ure):

Leaving the Fold: Candid Conversations with Inactive Mormons

Bait for Trout: Being the Confessions of an Unorthodox Angler

Fly Fishing for Sales (sample chapters follow this page. Coming in 2013)

Hawks and Roses Polio Boys (coming in 2013)

Hawk Lady (by Stellanie Ure with Jim Ure)

Comments? Visit our website: www.jimurebooks.com.

Sample Chapters
Fly Fishing for Sales
Coming Soon

Learn the Axioms of Selling Sharp Steel Hooks to Fish And You Can Make Big Money in Sales

By Jim Ure
www.jimurebooks.com

Catch and Release Means High-Ticket Sales—Again and Again.

All is fish that cometh to the net.
John Heywood, *Proverbs*, 1546

Trout laugh. I hear them laugh every time I make a mistake when casting a fly. I imagine them deep in their runs chuckling to themselves and daring me to come and get them. On the days when I am wise, they teach me how to become a better fisher. And when I make note of what happened and apply it to my business, I become a better salesman.

Laughing trout have taught me well over forty years of fishing and sales experience.

I now share with you the lessons I have learned and the mistakes I have made. Apply these lessons and you will become a Sales Superstar. If you can learn the axioms of selling sharp steel hooks to fish, you can sell anything.

Selling requires alertness, an agile and curious mind, exceptional knowledge of your product or service, and an awareness of the subtleties of change. Over the years, I have sold large and costly concepts to the shrewdest businesses in the United States, from Procter and Gamble to wily Hollywood film producers.

The toughest initial sale I ever made was to a group of skeptical bankers, who, like wary old trout, waited patiently, reticently. But once hooked, the bankers gave me their business for the next twenty years.

Another customer, a tough, bottom-line lawyer and owner of a bottled water business, resisted my lovely casts with hauteur. I kept returning, stalking him with new concepts until I watched his face brighten at an idea I had selected. It was exactly like presenting the right fly at the right moment. I had matched the proposal to his needs. I have been selling to this bottled water company for twenty-six years.

The Catch and Release Factor: If you want repeat sales, I say, "Never eat your customer." Like the trout I catch on dry flies, high-ticket buyers of intangibles will come back to purchase from you again and again if you maintain a light but steady touch. As the great fly fisherman Lee Wulff once said, "Trout are too valuable to eat." And so are your customers. That is why we catch and release.

Or as my brother and fishing partner Joe often reminds me: you can skin a sheep once but you can shear him again and again.

If you are selling high-ticket intangibles—stocks, insurance, phone service, advertising, software, or if you are

Fly Fishing For Sales

raising money for an art gallery or private school—you are selling thin air, blue sky, selling a chimera.

And it is very much like selling a tiny bit of artificial fluff, feathers, and sharp steel to a trout.

Masterly fly fishing for trout can be summed up in axioms that are applicable to selling—especially to selling high-ticket, expensive items. Learn them well and become the sales superstar that I know is within you.

One of my first jobs was as a copy boy at a daily newspaper. I sold my way from that position to being the paper's campus correspondent at the university I was attending; then I sold the editor on my ability to move to a staff writing job.

Newspaper reporting is exciting, but publishers realize that for most news writers the rewards are psychic, not financial. I grew frustrated working for peanuts.

The following spring, immediately after graduation from college, I moved into the business world and quickly learned that sales are the heartbeat of every business, the engine that drives all enterprise.

From the junior account assistant to the president of the company, everybody is in sales.

Certain principles apply to every kind of selling, be it selling a refrigerator, selling a private jet, or a selling a $50 million advertising campaign. A sales representative learns that the techniques for selling one product are much like selling another product.

Investment banker? Stock broker? Non-profit institution manager? You think you're not in sales? Wrong. If you are in any kind of business, account management, or fund-raising position today, you are in sales. And your high-ticket sales prospect offers special challenges:

- In high-ticket sales the prospects are fewer and hard to reach.
- The sales prospect is targeted by many salesmen and women, and there may be a parity between the products or services that he is offered.
- The sales prospect is jaded and hardened by sales representatives who have flailed their waters time and again, often with noisy inefficiency, perhaps even repelling the prospect and leaving the waters muddied.

Your window of opportunity is tight and narrow in high-ticket sales, and you must approach it with all the stealth and strategy of a dry fly fisherman.

It was one of those long waits between casts. I watched the morning breeze spangle the green water with dancing sunlight. I held my rod under my arm, enjoying the moment.

Fly fishing is a meditative art. The rhythm of casting serves as a pump to clear my mind of everything but the moment I'm in. Now I was still, and watching. I was waiting for a large trout to rise. Then I would stalk him to make my presentation.

As I waited, a knowing feeling overcame me. I knew instinctively that it was time to begin this book. Forty years was long enough to wait to create the allegories linking fly fishing with business success.

In one of the axioms in this book you will read how I made a sales presentation to the wrong guy. The weekend after this incident I went fishing. While on the river, I thought about my mistake. Later I wrote a note to myself and slipped it into a file marked "Fishing for Business."

Fly Fishing For Sales

Most of these axioms found their way to that file over all these years. They are all based on real situations. Some of the names and situations have been changed, for obvious reasons.

Share your sales rep and fishing stories with me? I want to hear them because I love being a salesman. Both of my grandfathers were salesmen and I wish they were here today so I could compare notes. Sales is a skill you can take anywhere. Even in the toughest of times. there is a job for you somewhere. Salesmen and saleswomen are practical, tough, yet always dreaming of a better future. They are the ultimate in optimism about the human condition. And salesmen and women are the most fun people I know. Send your feedback to via my website:
www.jimurebooks.com.

Now, get out your fly rod and get ready to be a better salesperson.

Axiom One: Embrace Your Business.

Surrender to the invigorating pull of the river. Be dazzled by the dancing sunlight on the water surface. See how it parts around rocks and branches, subtly muscling from bank-to-bank. Touch your fingers to the water and taste them. Marvel at the dimpled stillness where your trout rise to feed, wary, lovely, and worthy. This river of business is ever-changing, constantly renewing, forever exciting. And so is your business. Fall in love with it.

> *To business that we love we rise betime And go to't with delight.*
> —William Shakespeare, *Antony and Cleopatra*

A Forty Year Fascination with His Business

If you are like me you have doubtless fallen in love with a certain stretch of trout water. I love the Henry's Fork of the Snake River, for instance. It contains big fish. The landscape through which it flows is absolutely beautiful. It feels *right*. I go there again and again. A business should have that same hold on you.

Dr. Louis R. Curtis was retiring as president and CEO of a large and successful dairy products processing and packaging company with distribution throughout western America. I invited him to lunch.

Why have you been successful? I asked the gray-haired senior. (You should ask this question to every company executive you admire).

"It's all about falling in love with your business," he said.

I knew that, in the late 1930s, this company had been a small group of dairy farmers battling for their economic survival. Dr. Curtis had graduated from Cornell and had

Fly Fishing For Sales

brought his passion for dairy science to this group during the Great Depression.

"These dairymen were about to go under when I arrived," he said to me as he sipped his soup. "They were providing home milk delivery in glass bottles, using antiquated processing equipment. Worse, they didn't have a clue about modern dairy processing.

"The board of directors asked me if I would take a look at their business. The financial statements told me they were broke. Some of the farms were already in foreclosure. I wanted more than anything in the world to take this job, but I could not jeopardize my young family.

"Before making a decision I visited with their customers. The customers made one thing very clear: Milk was just milk. Price was everything in the Depression. I went into the markets and looked at the coolers with row after row of glass bottles of milk.

"Then it came to me. While at Cornell I had seen a company demonstrate a new way to package milk—some genius had invented a paper carton that would hold the stuff.

"I called the packaging company. I told them that if they would put their equipment in our plant at no cost to my farmers, we would put all our milk production in paper cartons.

"Then I went to the farmers and told them what I had done. If they wanted me, they would have to do as I told them, and that included converting to paper cartons. There always is resistance in any company to innovation, and someone asked, "What good will it do?"

"It will enable our customer to buy his milk at a market for a penny a quart less than they pay for it now," I told them. Finally, they agreed to go ahead with the paper carton idea.

"Three years later we had an astounding 50 per cent of the market. My farmers were making money. The competition tried to stop us by pricking pin holes in our cartons to turn them into leakers, but within another five years most dairies had converted to paper cartons. Then we had to deal with a new kind of competition.

"For the next 40 years it was like this. One moment success, another moment a challenge. Every moment was exciting for me. No two days were the same."

In today's market, some diaries are going back to glass bottles. Recycling gives now gives a dairy a point of superior exclusivity in a "green-minded" culture.

If you love your business, you tend it carefully and grow it like a garden.

Fly Fishing For Sales

Axiom Two: Observe with Detachment.

Balance your excitement with the clarity that comes with perspective and detachment. Walk the river in high water and in low. Lift its gravels. Sift it to know what grows in it. Mark its fluctuations. Find the places where the fish hold.

The most sensitive people ... are men of business and of the world, who argue from what they see and know, instead of spinning cobweb distinctions of what things ought to be.
—William Hazlitt *(1778-1830), "On the Ignorance of the Learned"*

Mark the Fluctuations

Fishing may be good, but keep an eye out for thunderstorms. A graphite rod attracts lightning.

You may become emotionally involved in your sales work yet you must maintain the detachment in order to provide yourself with the perspective to make good sales decisions.

You need to always be alert to the realities of the market, as was illustrated to me when I worked at Procter and Gamble in the Foods Division.

Our P&G cake mix group wanted to know the future of our business. At the time P&G's Duncan Hines Cake mixes had become the market leader, based on formulating a cake that was moister than those of the competition, and because of the remarkable and well-trained sales staff that spread across the country from our headquarters in Cincinnati.

The Food Products Division at P&G was supposedly the light of the future for the marketing giant.

What would the future for cake mixes be?

Fly Fishing For Sales

"You need to keep tabs on the fluctuations in the market, not just in your product," said Robert Kingsmith, a P&G exec as we entered the board room one morning to receive a presentation of the results of an extensive study by Simmons, a well-known and highly regarded research group.

Out came the charts as our presenter cleared his throat.

"There is good news and bad news," said the presenter. "We found that, while Procter and Gamble's market share of cake mixes has grown, the overall market for cake mixes is shrinking. There is a trend toward lighter desserts." He walked us through pages of charts. They clearly demonstrated a declining market.

It was on that day that P&G got the word that it might not want to stay in the cake mix business forever, and it might want to focus on other products with a greater promise of expanding markets. Eventually P&G divested itself of the Duncan Hines label, partly to allow its sales reps to focus on brands with growth potential.

Fly Fishing For Sales

Axiom Three: Risk It.

Wade. Fall in. Be swept away. Learn from your mistakes. Surrender to win.

A company must be flexible enough to attack itself with a new idea.
—Al Ries and Jack Trout, *The 22 Immutable Laws of Marketing*

Surrender to Win

After a month as a sales representative and some sales success, Mark thought he knew it all and now was trying to sell the lady of the house on his company's bottled water service.

He had told her about the product's clear superiority over that of the competition—it was pure spring water with fewer dissolved solids when compared to the competition's filtered tap water.

He had a demonstration that showed the health benefits of spring water—free of sodium, purity without chlorine. He argued that its cost was comparable to a filtration system and how water from a bottle provided a better product.

He showed her the bottled water dispenser, a model that would complement her modern kitchen, providing cold water for punch for the kids and hot water for things like tea and noodles.

The prospect, a woman homeowner, parried every thrust of the conversation with short ripostes of rejection, a simple "No."

In despair he finally said, "You aren't buying, are you?"

"No, I am not."

At this moment, he surrendered. "What's wrong with my spring water?"

"It's not the water. It's the dispenser. I have small children. I worry about them playing with it and burning themselves with hot water from the hot tap."

Mark had finally surrendered his ego and listened to his prospect. He left the lady and returned to the plant later in the day, telling Dave, his sales manager, of his rejection by the young mother.

"Oh," said the sales manager, brightening. "We have a dispenser model that is childproof. You have to move the taps backward and depress them before they will let the water flow. Little kids can play with them all day and nothing comes out of them."

Mark returned to the lady the next day and showed her the dispenser and its child-proof taps.

"Sign me up," said the lady.

Axiom Four: Expect To Win

You will bring a trout to the net. Hold that knowledge confidently.

When I feel like I will catch fish, I catch fish. When I feel doubtful, I never catch fish. Figure that out.

—John Young, violin maker and fisherman, personal commentary

Generating Confidence

The best salesman I ever met came into my office with his product, a financial service.

"You're a great salesman," I said, thinking of offering him a job at my own firm. "What's your secret?"

"I try to have confidence," he said modestly. "I spend 30 minutes every morning centering myself. I pray and meditate, asking for the will of a higher power to guide me.

"I ask that same higher power to provide me with confidence by keeping my expectations to a minimum. Projecting the outcome of a situation absolutely destroys my confidence because outcomes are always different than my expectations. Sometimes the real outcomes are better even than I could have imagined.

"So on my bathroom mirror I have a small sign that says:
'It ain't going to happen that way.'
"On my computer I have another small sign that says,
It ain't going to happen that way, either.'"

"I am confident I will sell you something, but I don't know what it will be. Really, it's a numbers game. You cast to enough fish, you catch one. So as long as I'm casting, I'm confident I will sell. In fishing, I never know if I'll hook a brown trout, a rainbow, a brook trout, or even a grayling."

He added, "Confidence comes to me with spiritual preparation and thorough product knowledge. I know that I am prepared to answer questions about my product because I have immersed myself in it. The sale comes, but never as I expected it to.

I made a note of his fishing metaphor. I also signed a contract with him. Couldn't touch him as an employee, however. He was making too much money where he was.

Axiom Five: Set No Time Limit

There is no season on your trout. If he resists in summer when the hatch is strong, return in winter and drift a nymph. Patience is the mark of wisdom.

Back in the fifties the Nash Rambler was America's first small car. But American Motors didn't have the money or the courage to hang in there long enough for the category to develop.
—Al Ries and Jack Trout, *The 22 Immutable Laws of Marketing*

Coyote Beer

Guy I knew loved making beer. He carefully brewed small batches of artisan beer that he would give to friends and serve at parties. He called it Coyote Beer. It was righteous beer, as all agreed, and he was often solicited to sell the stuff.

"If I could make a living at it, I would. But the big brewers would never let me in the market," he sighed. It was the early 1970s. He watched and waited.

In the 1980s, the big brewers continued consolidating, buying out small brewers until there were essentially just three giants: Anheuser Busch, Miller, and Coors.

Slowly things had changed. My guy's patience had seen a consolidation that resulted in disregarding the palates of many beer drinkers.

The big guys had become so big that little brewers creating small batches of artisan beer could develop niche markets. My guy thought maybe he could sneak in under the radar.

My guy put on his salesman's cap and visited his local supermarket. Sure, they would sell his beer. He went to other markets. He became involved in the local food movement.

Fly Fishing For Sales

He created a pub where he could showcase his beer. He created off-beat beer types beside Coyote Beer.

Today Coyote Beer is one of hundreds of small, profitable, and proliferating brewers who waited until the time was right. Coyote may get very big, and in time, another salesman with another idea for a beer, may come in under the radar to compete with that giant, Coyote Beer.

Enjoy these sample pages? Fly Fishing For Sales will soon be available at your favorite book sellers. For more information contact us through www.jimurebooks.com.

Made in the USA
Monee, IL
29 November 2021